George Stock

The Apology Of Plato, Parts I and II

George Stock

The Apology Of Plato, Parts I and II

ISBN/EAN: 9783741103490

Manufactured in Europe, USA, Canada, Australia, Japa

Cover: Foto ©ninafisch / pixelio.de

Manufactured and distributed by brebook publishing software (www.brebook.com)

George Stock

The Apology Of Plato, Parts I and II

Clarendon Press Series

THE
APOLOGY OF PLATO

WITH INTRODUCTION AND NOTES

BY

ST. GEORGE STOCK, M.A.
PEMBROKE COLLEGE

THIRD EDITION, REVISED

PART I.—INTRODUCTION AND TEXT

PREFACE TO THE FIRST EDITION.

BEING called upon to produce an edition of the Apology, I found myself embarrassed by the very abundance of material. For, unlike the Meno, the Apology had been amply edited in English. Indeed the only chance of imparting any distinctive character to a new edition seemed to lie in neglecting the labours of others and trusting to my own resources to produce such notes as a long experience in teaching suggested might be useful. This course appeared the more excusable as the edition asked for was required to be of a somewhat elementary character. Accordingly no commentator was consulted until my own notes were complete, Riddell only excepted, with whose views I was too familiar to be able to clear my mind of them, if I had wished to do so. It thus happens that a good deal of the common stock, especially in the way of illustrative references, has not been borrowed, but brought afresh. This, however, is a matter of very trifling importance to the reader, whose main concern is to find the matter at hand for his service. The other writers to whom I am bound to make acknowledgement for help here and there are Mr. Purves, who has included the whole of the Apology in his Selections from the Dialogues of Plato, the late Professor Wagner, and Mr. Louis Dyer, Assistant Professor in Harvard University, whose lucid Appendix on the Athenian Courts of Law has been of especial service. Mr. Adam's recent school edition, to which the present one must, to my regret, appear as a rival, I have never seen at all. It is perhaps superfluous to add that recourse has been had to such sources of information as Smith's Dictionary of Greek and Roman Biography and Mythology, the works of Zeller and the inexhaustible mine of learning contained in Grote's writings.

PREFACE.

Having acquitted myself of what may be called for distinction public obligations, I now turn to more private and personal ones. My old friend and school-fellow, the Rev. Robert L. Clarke, Fellow and Librarian of Queen's College, has once more exercised his patient kindness in revising my notes. How shall I thank him for the time he has spent upon me, or for the truly Socratic irony with which he convinced me of error, while seeming to defer to my arguments in defence of it! To Mr. Evelyn Abbott too, Fellow of Balliol College, I am indebted not only for the useful suggestions which his practical experience of editing enabled him to make, but also for having placed at my disposal some valuable matter, of which I have availed myself as freely as it was given. The text followed has again been that of K. F. Hermann.

8 MUSEUM VILLAS, OXFORD,
Sept. 1, 1887.

PREFACE TO THE SECOND EDITION.

In preparing this second edition of the Apology I have had the advantage of consulting Mr. J. Adam's excellent edition of the same classic in the Pitt Press Series. I am glad to find that our works need not be considered rivals, as his is intended for a higher class of readers than mine. The text in this edition has been brought into conformity, in all essentials, with that of Baiter, which is recognised by the University.

8 MUSEUM VILLAS, OXFORD,
July 30, 1890.

INTRODUCTION.

THE world will always be the better for the Apology of Socrates. It shows us philosophy tried before the bar of a passing public opinion, condemned to drink the bitter juice of the hemlock, and justified before the ages. It is an appeal from prejudice to reason, from seeming to being, from time to eternity. How often, when passion has subsided, does the better mind of man reject what man deliberately does in the name of God and goodness! As Anytus was leaving the court radiant with triumph, Socrates remarked, 'How miserable is this man, who seems not to know that, whichever of us has done the better and the nobler for all time, he it is who is the winner!' *Importance of the Apology.*

It is to Plato's Apology that the world indirectly owes the deep and enduring influence of Stoicism. For it was the reading of this little work which stirred up Zeno from his far home in Cyprus, and brought him to Athens to study philosophy.

The Apology is the natural introduction to the writings of Plato. Not only is it one of the simplest and easiest of his pieces, involving as it does no difficulties of argumentation, but it has the further advantage of giving us a full-length portrait of Socrates, in which the whole man is set vividly before us. In the dialogues we have Socrates at work on his mission: but the Apology lets us into the secret of what that mission was, and reveals to us the spirit in which Socrates undertook it. We see there the earnest thirst for truth, the dissatisfaction with received and unreasoned opinion, the incessant converse with men of all classes, the obstinate questioning of himself and others, the abnegation of all preten- *It forms the natural introduction to the study of Plato.*

sions to knowledge, the dialectical method, the negative result, the deep-seated persuasion of a personal guidance by some unseen intelligence, the unfaltering faith in goodness; nor are the lighter touches wanting—the raillery, the mock-solemnity, the delicious irony, the perfect politeness, the serene good humour.

Lost Socratic literature. The 'Socraticæ chartæ' were far more extensive than the remains which have come down to us. We cannot indeed quarrel with time, which has preserved to us all Plato: but still a great loss has been sustained. Of the innumerable works of Antisthenes[1], which made Timon call him 'an all-producing babbler,' not one has been spared to us. He was placed by ancient critics in the foremost rank of the Socratics, on a level with Plato and Xenophon. Of Alexamenus of Teos nothing more is known than that his were the first-written of the Socratic dialogues[2]. Among the other immediate disciples or friends of Socrates there were dialogues current in antiquity under the names of Aeschines, Aristippus, Bryson, Cebes, Crito, Eucleides, Glaucon, Phaedo, Simmias, and lastly of Simon the cobbler, to whose workshop Socrates used to resort, and who took notes of his discourses[3]. Amid this abundant Socratic literature, all of which owed its birth to the one originative impulse, there must have been much which would have helped us to bridge over the gulf between the Socrates of Plato and the Socrates of Xenophon. Aeschines in particular, owing to his lack of imagination, was supposed by some critics to have reflected more faithfully *The three* than anyone else the genuine mind of Socrates[4]. As it is,

---

[1] Diog. Laert. vi. §§ 15–18.   [2] Athen. 505 c

[3] On Antisthenes, see Diog. Laert. ii. § 47; on Alexamenus, Athen. 505 c, on Aeschines, Diog. Laert. ii. §§ 60, 61; on Aristippus, Athen. xi. 118 d, Diog. Laert. ii. §§ 83, 84, on Bryson, Athen. xi. 508 d, 509 c, with which cp. Xen. Conv. iv. § 63; on Cebes, one of whose three dialogues, the Πίναξ, is still extant, Diog. Laert. ii. § 125; on Crito, Diog. Laert. ii. § 121; on Eucleides, Diog. Laert. ii §§ 64, 108; on Glaucon and Simmias, Diog. Laert. ii § 124; on Simon the cobbler, Diog. Laert. ii §§ 122, 123.

[4] Aristeides Rhetor Orat. xlvi, p. 295, Dindorf.

INTRODUCTION. 7

however, we are reduced to three contemporary sources of information in endeavouring to estimate the real personality of Socrates—namely, the picture drawn of him by Xenophon, the picture drawn of him by Plato, and the picture drawn of him by Aristophanes.

pictures of Socrates, namely, those of Xenophon, Plato, Aristophanes.

Widely different as these three pictures are, they have yet no unlikeness which is fatal to the genuineness of any. You may always distort a countenance almost beyond the bounds of recognition by merely depressing some of the features without at all exaggerating the rest. Xenophon, the man of action, brings out into full relief the practical side of the mind of Socrates; the theoretical is sketched only in faint outline. We have a hint given us here and there of a style of discourse, which the biographer, absorbed in admiration of the moral and social qualities of his hero, did not care to record at length. To Plato, on the other hand, the thing of absorbing interest is the theoretical side of his master's mind, with which he has so interblended his own, that his very contemporaries did not seek to distinguish between the two. Socrates and Plato are like the married spirits seen by Swedenborg, who presented to the observer the appearance of one human being.

They are not really conflicting

Even the caricature of Socrates drawn in the Clouds of Aristophanes does not contradict the ideas we derive of him from elsewhere. Only we have now shifted to the point of view of the enemy. Instead of marvelling at the severity and subtlety of the mind which must and will see what can be said on both sides of a question, before it incline to either, we condemn the Sophist, who is upsetting all established notions, and whose whole skill is to 'make the worse appear the better reason.' From this it is an easy descent to represent him as a person of more than doubtful morality, whose society is contaminating his contemporaries from Euripides[1] downwards. Difficult as it is for us to realise that Socrates could ever have been a mark for righteous indignation, as we look back upon his figure, encircled with a halo through the vista of years, we must yet remember that this third picture

[1] Frogs, 1491.

of Socrates was the popular one, and that in his own lifetime he was numbered among the disreputable[1], and labelled 'dangerous.'

The Socrates of the Memorabilia.

As it is this third picture of Socrates which chiefly concerns the reader of the Apology, we will not dwell here upon the other two, nor seek to adjudge between their respective claims to authenticity. Certainly the sententious person described by Xenophon in the Memorabilia, who too often reminds us painfully of Mr. Barlow, does not seem likely to have stirred men's minds by his discourses, as we know that the real Socrates actually did above all talkers before or after him, one only excepted. It may be, as an ingenious friend has put it to me, that Socrates 'talked up to Plato and down to Xenophon;' but more likely Socrates was the same throughout, and the mental eye of Plato and Xenophon saw in him what it brought the power to see. The Memorabilia indeed contains nothing but what is edifying, and some things that are striking; but the mass of it is simply commonplace. We may grant that what is commonplace now was profound and original when it was first uttered, and that it is the triumph of truth to have become truism: but this will not avail us much, for a good deal of what the Memorabilia contains must, to adapt a vigorous phrase of Macaulay's, have been commonplace at the court of Chedorlaomer.

The Socrates of Xenophon's Symposium.

The sketch of Socrates in his lighter moments drawn by Xenophon in his Symposium approaches more nearly to Plato than anything in the Memorabilia. Xenophon's touch lacks the delicacy of Plato's, which redeems some of the features from coarseness: but we feel in reading the Symposium that we have essentially the same man before us as the Socrates of the Platonic dialogues.

Personality of Socrates.

How the personality of that man has stamped itself upon the world's memory! We can picture him now to ourselves as familiarly as if he had moved among us but yesterday—

[1] Charmides says in the Symposium of Xenophon (Xen. Conv. § 32), ἀλλὰ καὶ Σωκράτει, ὅτε μὲν πλούσιος ἦν, ἐλοιδόρουν με ὅτι συνῆν, νῦν δ' ἐπεὶ πένης γεγένημαι, οὐκέτι οὐδὲν μέλει οὐδενί.

the robust frame, the frank ugliness, of which his friends, if not himself, were vain, the Silenus-like features, the snub nose, the thick lips, the protruding eyes—a regular beauty, as he himself declared, if beauty is to be measured by utility; for his eyes enabled him to see round the corner, his nostrils were expanded to meet all odours, his nose had no useless bridge to interfere with seeing, his jaws were strong to bite, and his lips were soft to kiss[1]. We can fancy him starting from his humble home, shoeless and shirtless, as his manner was, except on some great occasion, when he wished to do honour to the banquet of a friend. He has risen betimes in the morning, and enjoyed the plain fare which a slave might have grumbled at; and now he is off to the walks or to the gymnasia, secretly glad perhaps to be relieved for a time from the excellent practice which Xanthippe afforded him in learning to bear patiently the humours of mankind. Later on in the day, when the market is filling, he will be sure to be there. for wherever men congregate, there Socrates finds the materials for study. He may unroll the volumes of antiquity at intervals with his disciples, seeking to cull from their pages some maxims which may be useful for life: but the real books of Socrates are 'the men in the city.' So devoted in fact is Socrates to this fascinating study of man, that he appears like a stranger beyond the city walls, and has to be enticed outside of them by Phaedrus with a book under his arm, like a donkey by a carrot. He might leave Athens on a religious mission, or at the call of duty, to serve with steady valour in the wars of his country; but would never be tempted away by the promptings of inclination. For what need had Socrates to leave Athens, 'the very prytaneum of wisdom,' to which all the most famous wits of the age were only too glad to come? It was there that his life's work lay, which he believed had been appointed him by God 'both by oracles and dreams, and in every way in which any divine dispensation had ever appointed anything to a man to do.'

[1] Xen. Conv. 1. §§ 5-7.

And what was this life's work? The queerest surely that was ever undertaken by mortal—but then Socrates was the queerest of mortals, as friends and foes alike declared; in fact half the secret of the mysterious charm which drew around Socrates a circle of devoted attendants, consisting of the keenest and brightest intellects of the age, lay in the fact that they had never seen or heard of anyone like him[1]. The work then to which Socrates conceived himself to be called was that of convincing all the glib talkers of the age —the statesmen, sophists, rhetoricians, poets, diviners, rhapsodes, and all the rest of them, that they really knew nothing of the things which they were talking about. For not one of them could define the art or science which he professed to practise or to teach; and Socrates considered that all true knowledge must rest upon general definitions[2]. It was the effort to apply this simple principle that led to the creation of the science of logic. And as the application was made exclusively to subjects connected with man, the διαλεκτική, which Socrates so incessantly practised, contained in germ ethics, politics, logic and metaphysics. Thus we see how the discourses of Socrates were the prolific seed-bed out of which sprang all subsequent Greek philosophy. It is not, however, with the philosophical importance of Socrates' conversation that we are here concerned, but with the practical effect produced by his ἔλεγχος, or method of cross-examination, upon the minds of his victims. That effect, it is scarcely necessary to state, took the form of an extreme exasperation, in spite of the polished urbanity with which the operation was performed; in spite also of the soothing profession, which invariably accompanied it, that Socrates was equally ignorant with his respondent, and was availing himself of his valuable assistance in the search for knowledge.

The picture that we have endeavoured to present of Socrates' personality is not complete, until we have added the crowning feature of all—the claim modestly but seriously

---

[1] Plat. Symp. 221 c.   [2] Xen. Mem. IV. 6, § 1.

advanced by this strange being that he was directly inspired by God. From his boyhood Socrates had been conscious of a singular experience, which appeared to mark him off from the rest of mankind. This was in an inner voice, which seemed to speak with him, and would check him suddenly when about to do or say something. To this voice Socrates yielded an unquestioning obedience, and was enabled by its aid to give wise advice to his friends with regard to the future —advice which they never refused to follow without subsequently regretting it [1].

Connected doubtless with this phenomenon were the strange fits of abstraction to which Socrates was liable at the most unexpected moments. His friends, who were acquainted with this peculiarity, made a point of not allowing him to be disturbed when he was in this condition. On one occasion, at Potidaea, Socrates is related to have stood thus in meditation for twenty-four hours, to the amazement of his fellow-soldiers, some of whom camped out all night from curiosity to see how long the fit of abstraction would continue. At sunrise Socrates said his prayers to the sun, and went off about his business [2]. *His fits of abstraction.*

Such was the man who, up to the age of seventy, played the part of a gadfly to the Athenians, settling down upon them morning, noon and night, pestering them with his awkward questions and bewildering them with his dialectic, until all their ideas seemed to be turned upside down; calling into question, always indirectly, and with the most provoking appearance of having reason upon his side, the value of their religion, the value of their morality, the value of their political institutions, the value of their professional employments and of their cherished aims in life—the value in short of everything except truth and goodness: for of the value of these things Socrates never doubted, nor allowed others to doubt. *His habit of calling everything into question.*

[1] Xen. Mem. i. 1, § 4, iv. 3, § 12, iv. 8, § 5; Apol. Soc. §§ 4, 13; Plato, Apol. 31 D, 40 B; Theaet. 151 A; Phaedrus 242 B, C; Rep. 496 C; Theag. 128 D—129 D
[2] Symp. 175 B, 220 C, D.

Public exasperation against him.

Human nature being what it is, we need not feel much surprised that the day of reckoning should have come at last. People might have put up with Socrates himself[1]; but, unfortunately, his example had raised a host of imitators. For the young men who had leisure to attend him, and who naturally belonged in the main to the upper classes, had begun to turn against their elders the weapons of negative dialectic, which they had learnt to use during their intercourse with Socrates. This was the thing which brought public indignation to a climax. There was an outcry raised that the young men were being ruined, and that the person who was ruining them was Socrates. It needed now only that someone should take the initiative in attacking him, for all classes in the community had been annoyed and offended in turn.

Anytus.

Prominent at this time (B.C. 399) among the leaders of the restored democracy was Anytus, who had fought and suffered in the cause of the people. We need not listen to the scandal of Scholiasts and of late Greek writers, by whom his character has been assailed. It is enough that by the confession of Plato, corroborated by the negative testimony of Xenophon, Anytus was a perfectly respectable person, and in fact a fairly favourable specimen of the democratic statesman. To this man Socrates had unfortunately given offence by saying that it ill became his position in the state to bring up his son to the family trade of a tanner. Anytus may have been animated to some extent by personal motives: but it is quite intelligible that he conceived himself to be acting on public grounds, and that he sincerely believed Socrates to be a very mischievous person. This conviction is not likely to have been diminished by the fact that the political leanings of Socrates were rather to the aristocratic side, as manifested by a theoretical admiration for the customs and institutions of Sparta[2]. Besides which, Critias, the bloodthirsty inaugurator of the recent reign of terror at Athens, had at one time been prominent among the dis-

---

[1] Euthyphro, 3 C. [2] Crito 52 E

ciples of Socrates, and some of the odium which his memory excited no doubt recoiled upon his former teacher.

Though Anytus was the prime mover in the matter, he was not the ostensible prosecutor of Socrates, that part being played by a young and comparatively obscure man, named Meletus, the son, as it would appear, of a well-known poet of the same name. A third person who took part in the prosecution was Lycon, a rhetorician. Thus the three accusers were representative of the outraged feelings and harassed interests of different classes in the community—Anytus taking up the quarrel of the manufacturers and politicians against Socrates, Lycon that of the rhetoricians, and Meletus that of the poets. *Meletus and Lycon*

But it is one thing to believe that a man's influence is mischievous in a community, and quite another to bring home to him a definite charge, which shall suffice to secure his condemnation. How then were his enemies to lay hold of Socrates, the spotless integrity of whose whole career did not seem to offer much handle to an accuser? The following considerations may help us partially to understand this question.

Philosophy up to this period had run wholly in the groove of physical inquiry, and, strange to say, had been thoroughly mechanical and materialistic in its tendencies, seeking to explain everything by evolution out of some material elements. We are apt to regard this as the final consummation of philosophy, but it was the first stage among the Greeks, which they outgrew with the advance of thought. It was so striking a novelty to proclaim that mind was necessary to arrange these elements into the organic whole of the universe, that Aristotle tells us that Anaxagoras, or whoever preceded him in doing so, appeared like the only sober man among drunkards[1]. Nevertheless Anaxagoras himself, who had made his home at Athens, had been indicted for impiety, in declaring the sun to be a material object, and had been obliged to take refuge at Lampsacus. Late writers tell us that Socrates had *State of philosophy before Socrates.*

Indictment of Anaxagoras for impiety. Relation o

[1] Metaphysics I 3, § 16.

Socrates to Anaxagoras been a pupil of Anaxagoras, and, after his condemnation, of his disciple Archelaus, with whom the Ionic school of physical philosophy came to a close[1]. We seem to gather however from Plato, that whatever acquaintance Socrates may have had with the doctrines of Anaxagoras was derived from reading. He is made to say in the Phaedo that the delight with which he at first hailed the teaching of Anaxagoras gave way subsequently to intense disappointment, when he found him deserting final for physical causes, and proving untrue to his own grand principle. For Socrates imagined he had found in Anaxagoras a guide who would conduct him on a royal road to the knowledge of nature If the universe were really constructed by mind, must it not be constructed in the best manner possible? And surely then the right method of studying nature was to seek to ascertain what was best and why. But Socrates found Anaxagoras, instead of pursuing this method, descanting, like the rest, upon air, fire and water, and in fact confounding the physical conditions with the real causes of phenomena[2]. Accordingly he abandoned Anaxagoras in disgust, and included him in his sweeping condemnation of the physicists generally as little better than madmen[3]. The discourses on

Influence of Socrates on physical science. nature recorded in the Memorabilia[4] are entirely on the lines indicated in the Phaedo. For Socrates *did* talk occasionally on nature as well as on man, and notwithstanding his disavowal of physical science, he has nevertheless powerfully influenced the world in this department no less than in ethics and in logic, though his influence has been in this case a retarding one. He was the parent of the teleological idea which maintained undisputed sway over men's minds until Bacon headed a reaction against it, and declared in favour of the pre-Socratics, who had contented themselves

The popu- with the 'how' without the 'why.' But the distinction be-

---

[1] Diog Laert. ii. §§ 16, 19, 23, 45, x. § 12, Euseh. Praep. Evang. x. 15, § 9, ed. Heinichen.
[2] Phaedo 97-99.
[3] Xen. Mem i. 1, §§ 11-13; iv. 7, § 6.
[4] Mem. i. 4 and iv. 13; cp Conv vii. § 4.

INTRODUCTION. 15

tween Socrates and the Ionic school, profound as it was in reality, was too subtle for the men who condemned him. The rough and ready syllogism of the popular judgment ran thus— *[lar confusion of him with the Physicists rendered possible an indictment for irreligion.]*

All who talk about nature are atheists.
Socrates talks about nature.
∴ Socrates is an atheist.

If, as was well known, Socrates claimed to hold communication with some higher power, this only constituted an aggravation of his offence. Here was a man who was ready to believe in anything except what he was expected to believe in! *[His claim to inspiration served only to aggravate his supposed offence.]*

A prosecution for heresy was no new thing at Athens, as we have seen already from the case of Anaxagoras. So far back as the year 431 B.C. a law had been carried by the rhetor Diopeithes εἰσαγγέλλεσθαι τοὺς τὰ θεῖα μὴ νομίζοντας ἢ λόγους περὶ τῶν μεταρσίων διδάσκοντας[1]. *[Prosecution for heresy no novelty.]*

And so it came to pass that the man who above all others in that age and country believed most profoundly in God was brought up before a public tribunal as an atheist. This was the first count in the indictment.

The natural sequel to a charge of irreligion is a charge of immorality. It was hopeless to fasten any such charge upon Socrates directly, for the blamelessness of his life was patent to everybody, and so it was represented that his society had a corrupting influence upon the young. This was the second count in the indictment. Such a charge was difficult to meet, while it gave ample room for the play of prejudice. The tyrants of the Oligarchy, who had reason to fear the influence of Socrates upon young and ardent spirits, had shown the way in this direction, in forbidding Socrates to converse with any man under thirty[2]. *[Charge of corrupting the young.]*

As the first count was one which might have been urged against any philosopher of the period, so the second was one which might have been urged against any of the Sophists, a class of professional teachers who supplied the place of *[Socrates assimilated to the Physicists on the one]*

---

[1] Plut. Peric. 169 D; cp. Arist. Wasps 380.
[2] Xen. Mem. 1. 2, § 35.

THE APOLOGY.

hand and the Sophists on the other.

university teachers among the Greeks, and from whom, outwardly at least, Socrates was only distinguished by the fact that he did not receive pay for his services or give regular lectures.

Terms of the indictment against him.

Behold then Socrates arraigned on the double charge of irreligion and immorality! The indictment, with that delightful simplicity which so favourably distinguishes Greek from English legal phraseology[1], was worded thus:—Ἀδικεῖ Σωκράτης, οὓς μὲν ἡ πόλις νομίζει θεοὺς οὐ νομίζων, ἕτερα δὲ καινὰ δαιμόνια εἰσφέρων· ἀδικεῖ δὲ καὶ τοὺς νέους διαφθείρων. Τίμημα θάνατος.

Technical name for it

As the offence with which Socrates was charged was not against any individual, but against the state, the proper technical term for the proceedings was γραφή, not δίκη, though in a looser sense δίκη was used for any legal case, and is in fact the term exclusively employed in this connection throughout the Apology of Xenophon. It was then a γραφὴ ἀσεβείας which was brought against Socrates.

Preliminary proceedings. Socrates summoned to appear before the King Archon.

We can imagine the dismay of Xanthippe when one spring[2] morning Meletus called at the door accompanied by two witnesses (κλητῆρες) to serve a summons upon Socrates, citing him to appear before the King Archon. This was the second of the nine archons, who represented the priestly functions of the original patriarchal monarchy, and had jurisdiction over all cases touching religion. The Ἄρχων βασιλεύς might have stopped proceedings, had he been so inclined. As he did not, the indictment was in due course posted up in some public place, and all the city knew that Socrates was to be tried for his life. The first proceedings were still before the King Archon. They were called the ἀνάκρισις[3], and consisted in part in the registration under oath of the prosecutor's indictment and the defendant's plea

The ἀνάκρισις.

---

[1] Compare for instance the will of Aristotle, Theophrastus, or one of the later Peripatetics, preserved by Diogenes, with the will of Shakespeare.

[2] The trial took place in the Attic month Munychion, corresponding to the latter part of April and the beginning of May.

[3] See a playful employment of the term in Xen Conv v. § 2

INTRODUCTION. 17

in answer to it. This was known as the ἀντωμοσία, or, more correctly, the διωμοσία, and the document itself, which contained the indictment and the plea in reply, was also called ἀντωμοσία[1]. It is during this preliminary stage of proceedings that we find Socrates in the Euthyphro The diviner of that name is surprised to find him quitting his usual haunts in the Lyceum, and resorting instead to the neighbourhood of the King's Porch.

And now the final stage has been reached. The case is not tried before the high court of Areiopagus, but before an ordinary δικαστήριον or Heliastic Court, consisting of the same mixed elements as the ἐκκλησία Out of the six thousand annually elected δικασταί some five hundred of his fellow-citizens are told off to try Socrates; and within the limits of a single day the temerity of a city mob will dispose of the life of one of the noblest of mankind. It is true that each of them has sworn a solemn oath that he will give an impartial hearing to prosecutor and defendant, and will not let himself be influenced by considerations extraneous to the case[2]: but this will scarcely avail to supply him with an enlightened mind and a calm judgment. *The Court.*

The time assigned for the trial is divided into three lengths, which are measured by the κλεψύδρα, or water-clock. The first of these lengths will be occupied by the speeches of the prosecutors, the second by the defence of the accused and the pleadings of his advocates (συνηγόροι), if he has any. After the speeches have been listened to, as far as tumultuous interruptions will allow, the jurors will declare their vote by secret ballot, and if the perforated balls (ψῆφοι) exceed the solid ones, Socrates will be condemned. Then the third length of time will be devoted to estimating the amount and kind of penalty that has been deserved[3]. For the proceedings fall under the head of δίκη or ἀγὼν τίμητος, in which it is left to the court to fix the penalty, instead of its *Division of the time assigned for the trial.*

Method of voting.

The case an ἀγὼν τίμητος.

---
[1] Theaet. 172 E.
[2] Demosthenes against Timocrates, p. 748, § 151.
[3] Ὅ τι χρὴ παθεῖν ἢ ἀποτῖσαι, Apol 36 B; cp. Xen. Conv. v. § 8.

B

being fixed beforehand by law, as in a δίκη ἀτίμητος, which required no assessment. Accordingly the prosecutor will speak again in favour of the penalty he has already named, and the convicted man will be allowed to plead for a diminution of it. The jurors will then decide between them, and the legitimate proceedings of the trial will be over If the prisoner is allowed to address the court further, it will be by an act of grace.

First length of the day Speeches for the prosecution.

Meletus opens the case for the prosecution, advancing to the raised platform (βῆμα), from which the speakers addressed the court He is followed by Lycon and Anytus, the latter of whom uses his influence to impress upon the minds of the jurors the danger of acquitting Socrates, now that proceedings have been allowed to be taken against him. For his acquittal would be such a triumph, and would give such an impetus to the fashion of imitating him, that the rising generation would be irretrievably ruined.

Our knowledge does not enable us to discriminate between the parts played by the various accusers, nor indeed to realise in any satisfactory manner on what lines the case for the prosecution was conducted. All that we can do is to put down a few points which we know to have been urged. We have seen already that there were two main counts in the indictment,

First Count. Charge of irreligion.

(1) Irreligion.
(2) Immoral influence.

With regard to the first count Socrates professes himself in doubt as to whether the accusers meant that he did not believe in gods at all, or only that he believed in different gods from those which were recognised by the city. This is a doubt which we must be content to share. If the remark addressed to the jurors by Meletus, about Socrates saying that the sun was a stone and the moon earth, is not a mere invention of Plato's, we may suppose that to some extent a line was followed similar to the gross mis-representation of the Clouds, in which Socrates is represented as having dethroned Zeus, and made 'Vortex' reign in his stead. But the main stress of the indictment, as is evident from the terms of it, must have fallen rather upon the impiety of which Socrates was supposed to be guilty, in exalting his private and personal source of inspiration over the public worship of his country. He was declared to be a daring innovator in religion, who held the time-honoured gods in contempt [1].

He would be a bold man who would undertake to say what Socrates really thought about Zeus and Hera, and the rest of the recognised deities of Greece. On the one hand the great philosopher was what would now-a-days be considered a very superstitious person. To say nothing of his inward monitor, he was ready to act on the strength of dreams, and had a robust faith in oracles, especially that of Delphi—a faith which could even survive the shock consequent upon his being told that he was the wisest of men. On the other hand we find in Xenophon clear expressions of a belief in one Supreme Being, the author and controller of the whole universe [2], which yet is held concurrently with a recognition of the many gods of Paganism, insomuch that monotheistic and polytheistic phraseology are mixed up in the same sentence.

Difficulty of determining the real belief of Socrates about religion.

A passage in the Phaedrus is interesting as bearing upon this subject. In reply to a question put by Phaedrus, as to what he thought of the story of Boreas and Oreithyia, Socrates declares that it would be easy enough for him to say with the clever that the girl was blown over a cliff by a gust of wind. But then logical consistency would require a similar rationalisation of innumerable other legends. He really had not time for a task of such appalling magnitude, and preferred to acquiesce in the current acceptance of the myths as they stood. There were mysteries enough in his own being fully to occupy all his attention [3]. Where, however, these myths ran counter to his notions of morality—and it was seldom that they did not—Socrates felt an ex-

---

[1] See Euthyphro, 3 B.
[2] Ὁ τὸν ὅλον κόσμον συντάττων τε καὶ συνέχων, Mem. iv. 4, § 13; cp i. 4, § 18.   [3] Phaedrus, 229 C–230 A.

treme repugnance to them. It is hinted in the Euthyphro[1] that this fact may have had something to do with his indictment for impiety.

His practical conformity with the religion of his country.

But whatever the opinions of Socrates may have been, there is no doubt at all about his practice. Accepting the principle laid down by the Delphic oracle[2], he thought it the part of a good citizen to conform to the religion of his country, and was scrupulous in so doing both in public and private life, holding a low opinion of those who did otherwise[3]. Everyone will remember his last words to Crito, charging him to sacrifice a cock to Aesculapius.

Second Count. Charge of immoral influence Special points urged.

Under the second count of the indictment it was urged that Socrates ridiculed the institutions of his country, declaring that it was absurd to elect magistrates by lot, when no one would care to entrust his life at sea to a pilot who had been chosen by that method. Such discourses, it was asserted, made the young men feel a contempt for the established constitution, and incited them to violence[4]. In proof of this pernicious influence it was pointed out how Critias and Alcibiades had been educated under Socrates[5].

Further it was maintained that Socrates inculcated disrespect to parents and relations generally by pointing out that mere goodwill was useless without knowledge. One did not consult one's relations in case of sickness or of legal difficulties, but the doctor or lawyer. The effect of such teaching, it was declared, was to make the associates of Socrates look so entirely to him, that no one else had any influence with them[6]. In the Apology of Xenophon this charge is specially ascribed to Meletus.

The only other point which we know to have been urged against Socrates was that he inculcated depravity by means of garbled citations from the poets[7]—that he quoted Hesiod's line[8],

---

[1] Euthyphro, 6 A. [2] Xen. Mem. i. 3, § 1; iv. 3, § 16.
[3] Mem. i. 3, § 1. [4] Mem. i. 2, § 9; cp iii 7, § 6.
[5] Mem. i. 2, § 12; cp. Plat. Apol. 33 B.
[6] Mem. i. 2, §§ 49, 51, 52. [7] Mem. i 2, §§ 56, 58, 59.
[8] Works and Days, 309.

INTRODUCTION.

'Έργον δ' οὐδὲν ὄνειδος, ἀεργίη δέ τ' ὄνειδος,

and drew from it the lesson that a man ought to be a πανοῦργος, or scamp who would do anything for gain; again that he was fond of quoting Homer[1] to show the different treatment meted out by Ulysses to the chiefs and the common people, drawing therefrom the inference that it was desirable to maltreat the humbler citizens This is plainly nothing but an appeal to the passions of the mob. Xenophon stops the quotation just short of the famous sentiment,

Οὐκ ἀγαθὸν πολυκοιρανίη· εἷς κοίρανος ἔστω,

of which Theophrastus says that it is the one line in Homer which 'the oligarchical man' is acquainted with. The political animus underlying so frivolous a charge is made even more transparent by Xenophon's reply. Xenophon is rather hard put to it to prove Socrates a good citizen from a democratic point of view[2]. He finds proof of this in the fact that Socrates never charged anyone a fee for conversing with him.

When the prosecutors had completed their indictment the first of the three lengths into which the juridical day was divided was at a close.

The water is now turned on for the defendant and his advocates. We gather from a passing expression in Xenophon[3] that Socrates had friends who spoke in his favour, but we know nothing of what they said. so that for us the second length is occupied solely by Socrates' own defence of himself. *Second length of the day.*

This defence was really made impromptu: for Socrates had twice been checked by his inward monitor when he endeavoured to prepare a reply beforehand[4]. The Apology of Plato, however, is marked by the same artistic grace which characterises all his work. It is elaborately constructed on *Socrates' defence really impromptu. Elaborate*

---

[1] Il ii. 188–192, 198–202.
[2] Δημοτικὸς καὶ φιλάνθρωπος, Mem. i. 2, § 60.
[3] Apol Soc. § 22.   [4] Mem. iv. 8, § 5; Apol. Soc § 4.

THE APOLOGY.

construction of Plato's Apology. Its divisions

the forensic type, of which it is at once a parody and a criticism. It is divided into three parts, of which the first only constitutes the defence proper. The second is the ἀντιτίμησις, or counter-assessment of the penalty, and belongs to the third length of the juridical day. The third part consists of some last words addressed by the prisoner to the court after his conviction. It is not necessary here to enter into details with regard to the contents of these several parts. The reader will find a scheme of the speech prefixed to the text and a detailed analysis interwoven with it. Suffice it to say that the subdivisions of the defence are completely in accordance with rhetorical precedent. The citation of witnesses is also imitated[1], a proceeding during which the water was stopped, and even the common rhetorical challenge to opponents is reproduced, to bring forward witnesses, if they can, during the time allotted to the speaker[2]. In place of the usual impassioned peroration, Socrates substitutes a dignified refusal to throw himself in any way upon the mercy of his judges.

Imitation of forensic forms.

Condemnation of Socrates.

When the pleadings in defence were concluded, the court proceeded to give their verdict, and condemned Socrates by 281 votes against 220. Considering the long and deeply-rooted prejudice which existed against Socrates at Athens, we can well believe that many honest and ignorant men among the dicasts went home to their suppers that day with the comfortable assurance that they had conscientiously discharged their duty as good citizens. There is no doubt, however, but that to some extent the verdict was influenced by irritation at the unaccustomed tone adopted by the defendant, who addressed his judges, as Cicero says[3], not as a suppliant or prisoner, but as a teacher or master.

Third length of the day. The Counter-assessment

The third length of the day was begun by a speech on the part of the prosecution in advocacy of the death-penalty. Then Socrates rose to present his estimate of the treatment he deserved to suffer, which was support for the rest of his days in the Prytaneum. If the judges had been annoyed before,

[1] 19 D, 21 A, 32 E.   [2] 34 A.   [3] Cic. de Oratore, 1. 54.

they were utterly exasperated now, and the death-penalty was confirmed by eighty additional votes[1]. *Ratification of the death-penalty.*

After the informal delivery of a short address by the condemned prisoner to the court nothing remained but for the officer of the Eleven to lead off Socrates to the adjacent prison, where the dialogue of the Phaedo again takes him up. And so that crime was committed, which, owing to the lustre of its victim, has left a lasting stain upon the name of Athens—the one city in all the Hellenic world which had most reason to pride itself upon its tolerance.

It has been remarked that the Platonic Apology resembles in a certain respect the famous speech of Demosthenes on the Crown, namely, that in both the formal answer to the indictment is thrown into the middle, and extraneous matters, which are more vital to the real issue, are brought to the front, and again insisted upon at the close. We have the key to this treatment in the words put into Socrates' mouth by Plato, that it is not Meletus or Anytus he has to fear, but the prejudice and envy of the multitude[2]. Accordingly we find the actual indictment treated so carelessly by Socrates that in his citation of it the order of the counts is reversed, and the charge of perverting the youth is dealt with before the charge of irreligion. The latter accusation indeed is never really answered at all—and rightly so, for if Socrates' life was not an answer to it, any other must have been felt to be idle and derogatory. *Comparison between the Apology and the speech of Demosthenes on the Crown. Careless treatment in the Apology of the technical indictment.*

Few will deny that the Platonic Apology is in every way worthy of the occasion and the man. How far it represents the actual words of Socrates before his judges is a question which it would be vain to argue a priori, by an appeal to the general fitness of things. But the historical method can to a certain extent be applied here. Reference has already been made to the Apology of Xenophon—a little work which it is the fashion to set down as a forgery, because there is scarcely anything in it which is not also contained in the Memorabilia: as if it were in any way improbable that a *How far can Plato's Apology be considered historical? The Apology of Xenophon.*

---

[1] Diog. Laert. ii. § 42.   [2] 28 A.

writer should cast the same matter at different times into slightly different moulds, or that even a rejected sketch, supposing it to be such, by an author so highly esteemed as Xenophon should have been carefully preserved.

Xenophon's authority for his version of Socrates' speech.

Xenophon himself returned from the expedition which has immortalised his name just too late to support his revered master on his trial; but he derived his information with regard to the closing scenes of Socrates' life from Hermogenes, the son of Hipponicus and brother of the wealthy Callias[1]. Hermogenes was an attached friend of Socrates, and is mentioned in the Phaedo as having been present at his death.

Analysis of Xenophon's Apology.

To turn from Plato to Xenophon is indeed a fall! The Socrates of the latter is so prosy and self-complacent that we cannot wonder if he irritated his judges. The whole impression produced on the mind by the piece is different from that with which one rises from Plato's Apology; and yet, on examining into details, one is surprised to find what resemblances it offers. The amount both of resemblance and difference will be manifest from a brief analysis of its contents.

The Apology of Xenophon then falls into the same three parts as that of Plato—

I. The Defence proper.
II. The Counter-assessment.
III. The Last Words.

I. The Defence proper, which grapples directly with the terms of the indictment, is sub-divided into two parts, in which the counts are taken in the accuser's order, dealing

(1) with the charge of irreligion;
(2) with the charge of immorality.

(1) The charge of downright irreligion is met by Socrates by an appeal to his habitual conformity with the public worship of his country; and the secondary one of innovation in religious matters by his assimilating the δαιμόνιον to divination generally. Under this head Socrates takes occasion

---

[1] Mem. iv. 8, § 4; Apol. Soc. § 1.

to vaunt of his prophetic powers, as a proof of the favour in which he is held by the gods; and then tells the story of Chaerephon consulting the oracle about him[1]. The reply of the oracle, as here given, is that there is no one more free, just or temperate than Socrates—a claim which the defendant then proceeds to vindicate in detail by extolling his own virtue under each head

(2) The refutation of the second count takes the form of a dialogue with Meletus[2]. Socrates challenges his accuser to produce a single person who has been demoralised by his society[3]. The special charge of inculcating disrespect to parents, which was prompted by jealousy of Socrates' influence, is met by his claiming to be an expert on the subject of education, as much as a doctor was on medicine.

II The Counter-assessment, it must be confessed, is like the famous chapter on snakes in Iceland. The proposal about the Prytaneum is absent, and we are told that Socrates neither suggested any diminution of the penalty himself nor allowed his friends to do so. It would seem, however, that he must have spoken a few words at this stage of the proceedings, in order to explain the grounds of his refusal to take the usual course, which were that he considered it tantamount to pleading guilty.

III. In the Last Words Socrates refers to perjury on the part of the witnesses against him, dwells on the wickedness of his accusers[4], and denies that the case is proven against him. He has not attempted to dethrone Zeus and Hera, nor corrupted the young, but set them a wholesome example of plain living. He comforts himself by the case of Palamedes[5], and ends by declaring that all time will witness to his righteousness.

The Apology of Xenophon does not claim to be an exhaustive report of the defence of Socrates. Even at the date of its composition what Socrates really said was matter

Xenophon's Apology

---

[1] Cp. Plat. Apol. 21. [2] Cp. Plat. Apol. 24–27.
[3] Cp. Plat. Apol. 33 D—34 C.
[4] Cp. 39 B. [5] Cp. 41 B.

does not claim to be exhaustive. Other Apologies.

for critical investigation. The author of it tells us that others had written on the same subject, and as all agreed about the high tone (μεγαληγορία) adopted by Socrates, he presumes that this was characteristic of the real defence. Among these 'others' Plato may be included, as Xenophon and he seem to have entered into a tacit agreement to ignore one another[1].

The story is well known how the great orator Lysias presented Socrates with a speech admirably adapted to conciliate the favour of his judges, which was admired by Socrates, but declined with thanks on the ground that it would be as inappropriate to him as fine shoes or cloaks[2]. On the other hand the sophist and rhetorician Polycrates, after the death of Socrates, composed an accusation against him, which was mistaken subsequently for the real speech delivered at the trial[3].

Even after the generation which witnessed the trial of Socrates had passed away, echoes of the event still rang on the air, and men exercised their wits in composing his apology. Theodectes, the friend of Aristotle, and a famous orator and dramatic writer of his day, composed an apology of Socrates[4]; as also did Demetrius Phalereus, the accomplished disciple of Theophrastus[5].

Date of the Apology indeterminable.
Its affinities with other Platonic works.

To return now to Plato's Apology—the date of its composition is a question which we have no means of determining. As to its affinities with other works of Plato, it presents a superficial resemblance to the Menexenus and a real resemblance to the Gorgias.

In the Menexenus, as in the Apology, Plato has given a specimen of what he might have done in the way of

---

[1] The name of Plato is only once mentioned by Xenophon, namely in Mem. iii 6, § 1; that of Xenophon by Plato never. This silence was ascribed by the ancients to jealousy. See on this subject Athen. xi 504 e—505 b, Diog Laert. i. § 34

[2] Cic. de Oratore, i 54; Val Max vi. 4, Extern 2; Quint. ii. 15, § 30; xi 1, § 11; Diog. Laert. ii. § 40

[3] Quint. ii. 17. § 4; iii. 1, § 11, Diog Laert. ii. § 38.

[4] Arist Rhet ii 23, § 13.   [5] Diog. Laert. ix. §§ 37, 57.

rhetoric, had he cared to desert his favourite dialectic. The Apology reflects, while it exalts, the pleadings of the law-courts; the Menexenus in like manner imitates the funeral orations which formed an important feature in public life at Athens. But in the Menexenus we have a speech within a dialogue; while in the Apology we have a dialogue within a speech.

The Apology compared with the Menexenus.

In the Gorgias we have the same sharp contrast drawn between the world's way and the way of philosophy. The Gorgias contains the prophecy of which the Apology is the fulfilment. In that dialogue Callicles, the man of the world, warns Socrates with contemptuous good-nature, that if he persists in continuing into mature age the study of philosophy, which is becoming enough in youth, he will unfit himself for converse with mankind, and, owing to his neglect of the rhetoric of the law-courts, will lay himself at the mercy of the meanest accuser who may choose to bring against him a capital charge[1]. Socrates admits that this may very possibly be the case, but contends that it is quite a secondary consideration, the first requisite for man's true welfare being to avoid committing injustice, the second only to escape suffering it. He contends that, in pursuing his appointed calling of philosophy, he is the only real politician of his time, since his words are not meant to give men pleasure, but to do them good. As this object necessarily involves his saying a great many disagreeable things, he is no more likely to fare well in a law-court than a doctor would be likely to come off triumphant, if tried before a jury of children, at the instance of the pastry-cook.

The Apology compared with the Gorgias.

If it be permissible to add one more suggestion to the many conflicting views that have been held as to the main object of the Gorgias, we might say that in the following words, more than in any other, we have an embodiment of Plato's motive in composing that dialogue—εἰ δὲ κολακικῆς ῥητορικῆς ἐνδείᾳ τελευτῴην ἔγωγε, εὖ οἶδα ὅτι ῥᾳδίως ἴδοις ἄν με φέροντα τὸν θάνατον[2].

Motive of the Gorgias.

---

[1] Gorg. 486 A, B.   [2] Gorg. 522 D, E.

The Gorgias is an earnest defence of that uncompromising spirit which rendered it impossible for Socrates to conciliate his judges at the expense of truth, which made him prefer 'to die as Socrates than to live as Lysias,' which prompted him to forego the remainder of his life rather than sully the past, and, at the cost of a few short years of decaying faculties, to purchase a life which has triumphed over time.

SCHEME OF THE SPEECH.

                              PAGE

I. THE DEFENCE PROPER, 17 A–35 D
    1. The Exordium, 17 A–18 A 31
    2. The Statement, 18 A–19 A 32
    3. The Refutation, 19 A–28 A 34
       a Defence against vague popular prejudice, 19 A–24 B 34
       b. Defence against the specific indictment, 24 B–28 A 41
    4. The Digression—A defence by Socrates of his life
       generally, 28 A–34 B 47
    5. The Peroration, 34 B–35 D 57
II. THE COUNTER-ASSESSMENT, 35 E–38 C . . 59
III. THE LAST WORDS, 38 C–42 A.
       a. Address to the condemning jurors, 38 C–39 E . 63
       b. Address to the acquitting jurors, 39 E–42 A . . 65

ΑΠΟΛΟΓΙΑ ΣΩΚΡΑΤΟΥΣ.

I. THE DEFENCE PROPER.

1. The Exordium, 17 A–18 A.

Do not be misled by the assertion of my accusers that I am skilled in speech. On the contrary I must ask you to pardon the manner of my defence, which is due to inexperience.

Ὅ τι μὲν ὑμεῖς, ὦ ἄνδρες Ἀθηναῖοι, πεπόνθατε ὑπὸ τῶν ἐμῶν κατηγόρων, οὐκ οἶδα· ἐγὼ δ᾽ οὖν καὶ αὐτὸς ὑπ᾽ αὐτῶν ὀλίγου ἐμαυτοῦ ἐπελαθόμην· οὕτω πιθανῶς ἔλεγον. καίτοι ἀληθές γε, ὡς ἔπος εἰπεῖν, οὐδὲν εἰρήκασι. μάλιστα δὲ αὐτῶν ἓν ἐθαύμασα τῶν πολλῶν ὧν ἐψεύσαντο, τοῦτο ἐν ᾧ ἔλεγον ὡς χρὴ ὑμᾶς εὐλαβεῖσθαι, μὴ ὑπ᾽ B ἐμοῦ ἐξαπατηθῆτε, ὡς δεινοῦ ὄντος λέγειν. τὸ γὰρ μὴ αἰσχυνθῆναι, ὅτι αὐτίκα ὑπ᾽ ἐμοῦ ἐξελεγχθήσονται ἔργῳ, ἐπειδὰν μηδ᾽ ὁπωστιοῦν φαίνωμαι δεινὸς λέγειν, τοῦτό μοι ἔδοξεν αὐτῶν ἀναισχυντότατον εἶναι, εἰ μὴ ἄρα δεινὸν καλοῦσιν οὗτοι λέγειν τὸν τἀληθῆ λέγοντα· εἰ μὲν γὰρ τοῦτο λέγουσιν, ὁμολογοίην ἂν ἔγωγε οὐ κατὰ τούτους εἶναι ῥήτωρ. οὗτοι μὲν οὖν, ὥσπερ ἐγὼ λέγω, ἤ τι ἢ οὐδὲν ἀληθὲς εἰρήκασιν· ὑμεῖς δ᾽ ἐμοῦ ἀκούσεσθε πᾶσαν τὴν ἀλήθειαν. οὐ μέντοι μὰ Δί᾽, ὦ ἄνδρες Ἀθηναῖοι, κεκαλλιεπημένους γε λόγους, ὥσπερ οἱ τούτων, ῥήμασί τε C καὶ ὀνόμασιν, οὐδὲ κεκοσμημένους, ἀλλ᾽ ἀκούσεσθε εἰκῇ λεγόμενα τοῖς ἐπιτυχοῦσιν ὀνόμασι· πιστεύω γὰρ δίκαια εἶναι ἃ λέγω, καὶ μηδεὶς ὑμῶν προσδοκησάτω ἄλλως· οὐδὲ γὰρ ἂν δήπου πρέποι, ὦ ἄνδρες, τῇδε τῇ ἡλικίᾳ ὥσπερ μειρακίῳ πλάττοντι λόγους εἰς ὑμᾶς εἰσιέναι. καὶ μέντοι καὶ πάνυ, ὦ ἄνδρες Ἀθηναῖοι, τοῦτο ὑμῶν δέομαι καὶ παρίεμαι· ἐὰν διὰ τῶν αὐτῶν λόγων ἀκούητέ μου ἀπολογουμένου, δι' ὧνπερ εἴωθα λέγειν καὶ ἐν ἀγορᾷ ἐπὶ τῶν τραπεζῶν, ἵνα ὑμῶν πολλοὶ ἀκηκόασι, καὶ ἄλλοθι, μήτε D θαυμάζειν μήτε θορυβεῖν τούτου ἕνεκα. ἔχει γὰρ οὑτωσί. νῦν ἐγὼ πρῶτον ἐπὶ δικαστήριον ἀναβέβηκα, ἔτη γεγονὼς ἑβδομήκοντα· ἀτεχνῶς οὖν ξένως ἔχω τῆς ἐνθάδε λέξεως. ὥσπερ οὖν ἄν, εἰ τῷ ὄντι ξένος ἐτύγχανον ὤν, ξυνεγιγνώσκετε δήπου ἄν μοι, εἰ ἐν ἐκείνῃ τῇ φωνῇ τε καὶ τῷ τρόπῳ ἔλεγον, ἐν οἷσπερ ἐτεθράμμην, καὶ δὴ καὶ νῦν 18 τοῦτο ὑμῶν δέομαι δίκαιον, ὥς γ' ἐμοὶ δοκῶ, τὸν μὲν τρόπον τῆς λέξεως ἐᾶν· ἴσως μὲν γὰρ χείρων, ἴσως δὲ βελτίων ἂν εἴη· αὐτὸ δὲ τοῦτο σκοπεῖν καὶ τούτῳ τὸν νοῦν προσέχειν, εἰ δίκαια λέγω ἢ μή· δικαστοῦ μὲν γὰρ αὕτη ἀρετή, ῥήτορος δὲ τἀληθῆ λέγειν.

2. The Statement, 18 A-19 A.

There are two classes of accusers, those who have maligned me all my life, and those who now indict me. Both must be answered, and the time is short: but let the law be obeyed.

Πρῶτον μὲν οὖν δίκαιός εἰμι ἀπολογήσασθαι, ὦ ἄνδρες Ἀθηναῖοι, πρὸς τὰ πρῶτά μου [ψευδῆ] κατηγορημένα καὶ τοὺς πρώτους κατηγόρους, ἔπειτα δὲ πρὸς τὰ ὕστερα καὶ τοὺς ὑστέρους. ἐμοῦ γὰρ πολλοὶ κατήγοροι γεγόνασι B πρὸς ὑμᾶς καὶ πάλαι πολλὰ ἤδη ἔτη καὶ οὐδὲν ἀληθὲς λέγοντες, οὓς ἐγὼ μᾶλλον φοβοῦμαι ἢ τοὺς ἀμφὶ Ἄνυτον, καίπερ ὄντας καὶ τούτους δεινούς· ἀλλ' ἐκεῖνοι δεινότεροι, ὦ ἄνδρες, οἳ ὑμῶν τοὺς πολλοὺς ἐκ παίδων παραλαμβάνοντες ἔπειθόν τε καὶ κατηγόρουν ἐμοῦ μᾶλλον οὐδὲν ἀληθές, ὡς ἔστι τις Σωκράτης, σοφὸς ἀνήρ, τά τε μετέωρα φροντιστὴς καὶ τὰ ὑπὸ γῆς ἅπαντα ἀνεζητηκὼς καὶ C τὸν ἥττω λόγον κρείττω ποιῶν. οὗτοι, ὦ ἄνδρες Ἀθηναῖοι, οἱ ταύτην τὴν φήμην κατασκεδάσαντες, οἱ δεινοί εἰσί μου κατήγοροι· οἱ γὰρ ἀκούοντες ἡγοῦνται τοὺς ταῦτα ζητοῦντας οὐδὲ θεοὺς νομίζειν. ἔπειτά εἰσιν οὗτοι οἱ κατήγοροι πολλοὶ καὶ πολὺν χρόνον ἤδη κατηγορηκότες, ἔτι δὲ καὶ ἐν ταύτῃ τῇ ἡλικίᾳ λέγοντες πρὸς ὑμᾶς, ἐν ᾗ ἂν μάλιστα ἐπιστεύσατε, παῖδες ὄντες, ἔνιοι δ' ὑμῶν καὶ μειράκια, ἀτεχνῶς ἐρήμην κατηγοροῦντες ἀπολογουμένου οὐδενός. ὃ δὲ πάντων ἀλογώτατον, ὅτι οὐδὲ τὰ ὀνόματα D οἷόν τε αὐτῶν εἰδέναι καὶ εἰπεῖν, πλὴν εἴ τις κωμῳδιοποιὸς τυγχάνει ὤν· ὅσοι δὲ φθόνῳ καὶ διαβολῇ χρώμενοι ὑμᾶς ἀνέπειθον, οἱ δὲ καὶ αὐτοὶ πεπεισμένοι ἄλλους πείθοντες, οὗτοι πάντες ἀπορώτατοί εἰσιν· οὐδὲ γὰρ ἀναβιβάσασθαι οἷόν τ' ἐστὶν αὐτῶν ἐνταυθοῖ οὐδ' ἐλέγξαι οὐδένα, ἀλλ' ἀνάγκη ἀτεχνῶς ὥσπερ σκιαμαχεῖν ἀπολογούμενόν τε καὶ ἐλέγχοντα μηδενὸς ἀποκρινομένου. ἀξιώσατε οὖν καὶ ὑμεῖς, ὥσπερ ἐγὼ λέγω, διττούς μου τοὺς κατηγόρους γεγονέναι, ἑτέρους μὲν τοὺς ἄρτι κατηγορήσαντας, ἑτέρους E δὲ τοὺς πάλαι, οὓς ἐγὼ λέγω. καὶ οἰήθητε δεῖν πρὸς ἐκείνους πρῶτόν με ἀπολογήσασθαι· καὶ γὰρ ὑμεῖς ἐκείνων πρότερον ἠκούσατε κατηγορούντων, καὶ πολὺ μᾶλλον ἢ τῶνδε τῶν ὕστερον. εἶεν· ἀπολογητέον δή, ὦ ἄνδρες Ἀθηναῖοι, 19 καὶ ἐπιχειρητέον ὑμῶν ἐξελέσθαι τὴν διαβολήν, ἣν ὑμεῖς ἐν πολλῷ χρόνῳ ἔσχετε, ταύτην ἐν οὕτως ὀλίγῳ χρόνῳ. βουλοίμην μὲν οὖν ἂν τοῦτο οὕτω γενέσθαι, εἴ τι ἄμεινον καὶ ὑμῖν καὶ ἐμοί, καὶ πλέον τί με ποιῆσαι ἀπολογούμενον· οἶμαι δὲ αὐτὸ χαλεπὸν εἶναι, καὶ οὐ πάνυ με λανθάνει οἷόν ἐστιν. ὅμως δὲ τοῦτο μὲν ἴτω ὅπῃ τῷ θεῷ φίλον, τῷ δὲ νόμῳ πειστέον καὶ ἀπολογητέον.

3. The Refutation, 19 A-28 A.

(a) Defence against vague popular prejudice.

I am no scientific atheist, nor do I educate men for money. Happy he who for the sum of £20 or so can impart the science of living well!

The charge brought by popular prejudice formulated.

Ἀναλάβωμεν οὖν ἐξ ἀρχῆς, τίς ἡ κατηγορία ἐστίν, ἐξ ἧς ἡ ἐμὴ διαβολὴ γέγονεν, ᾗ δὴ καὶ πιστεύων Μέλητός B με ἐγράψατο τὴν γραφὴν ταύτην. εἶεν· τί δὴ λέγοντες διέβαλλον οἱ διαβάλλοντες; ὥσπερ οὖν κατηγόρων τὴν ἀντωμοσίαν δεῖ ἀναγνῶναι αὐτῶν· Σωκράτης ἀδικεῖ καὶ περιεργάζεται ζητῶν τά τε ὑπὸ γῆς καὶ οὐράνια, καὶ τὸν ἥττω λόγον κρείττω ποιῶν, καὶ ἄλλους ταὐτὰ ταῦτα διδάσκων. τοιαύτη τίς ἐστι· ταῦτα γὰρ ἑωράτε καὶ αὐτοὶ C ἐν τῇ Ἀριστοφάνους κωμῳδίᾳ, Σωκράτη τινὰ ἐκεῖ περιφερόμενον, φάσκοντά τε ἀεροβατεῖν καὶ ἄλλην πολλὴν

Refutation of it.

φλυαρίαν φλυαροῦντα, ὧν ἐγὼ οὐδὲν οὔτε μέγα οὔτε σμικρὸν πέρι ἐπαΐω. καὶ οὐχ ὡς ἀτιμάζων λέγω τὴν τοιαύτην ἐπιστήμην, εἴ τις περὶ τῶν τοιούτων σοφός ἐστι· μή πως ἐγὼ ὑπὸ Μελήτου τοσαύτας δίκας φύγοιμι· ἀλλὰ γὰρ ἐμοὶ τούτων, ὦ ἄνδρες Ἀθηναῖοι, οὐδὲν μέτεστι. μάρτυρας δ᾽ αὐτοὺς ὑμῶν τοὺς πολλοὺς παρέχομαι, καὶ ἀξιῶ D ὑμᾶς ἀλλήλους διδάσκειν τε καὶ φράζειν, ὅσοι ἐμοῦ πώποτε ἀκηκόατε διαλεγομένου· πολλοὶ δὲ ὑμῶν οἱ τοιοῦτοί εἰσι· φράζετε οὖν ἀλλήλοις, εἰ πώποτε ἢ σμικρὸν ἢ μέγα ἤκουσέ τις ὑμῶν ἐμοῦ περὶ τῶν τοιούτων διαλεγομένου· καὶ ἐκ τούτου γνώσεσθε ὅτι τοιαῦτ᾽ ἐστὶ καὶ τἆλλα περὶ ἐμοῦ ἃ οἱ πολλοὶ λέγουσιν.

Ἀλλὰ γὰρ οὔτε τούτων οὐδέν ἐστιν, οὐδέ γ᾽ εἴ τινος ἀκηκόατε ὡς ἐγὼ παιδεύειν ἐπιχειρῶ ἀνθρώπους καὶ χρήματα πράττομαι, οὐδὲ τοῦτο ἀληθές. ἐπεὶ καὶ τοῦτό E

The Sophists.

γέ μοι δοκεῖ καλὸν εἶναι, εἴ τις οἷός τ᾽ εἴη παιδεύειν

ἀνθρώπους ὥσπερ Γοργίας τε ὁ Λεοντῖνος καὶ Πρόδικος ὁ Κεῖος καὶ Ἱππίας ὁ Ἠλεῖος. τούτων γὰρ ἕκαστος, ὦ ἄνδρες, [οἷός τ᾽ ἐστὶν] ἰὼν εἰς ἑκάστην τῶν πόλεων τοὺς νέους, οἷς ἔξεστι τῶν ἑαυτῶν πολιτῶν προῖκα ξυνεῖναι ᾧ ἂν βούλωνται, τούτους πείθουσι τὰς ἐκείνων ξυνουσίας 20 ἀπολιπόντας σφίσι ξυνεῖναι χρήματα διδόντας καὶ χάριν προσειδέναι. ἐπεὶ καὶ ἄλλος ἀνήρ ἐστι Πάριος ἐνθάδε σοφός, ὃν ἐγὼ ᾐσθόμην ἐπιδημοῦντα· ἔτυχον γὰρ προσελθὼν ἀνδρὶ ὃς τετέλεκε χρήματα σοφισταῖς πλείω ἢ ξύμπαντες οἱ ἄλλοι, Καλλίᾳ τῷ Ἱππονίκου· τοῦτον οὖν ἀνηρόμην — ἐστὸν γὰρ αὐτῷ δύο υἱέε — ὦ Καλλία, ἦν δ᾽ ἐγώ, εἰ μέν σου τὼ υἱέε πώλω ἢ μόσχω ἐγενέσθην, εἴχομεν ἂν αὐτοῖν ἐπιστάτην λαβεῖν καὶ μισθώσασθαι, ὃς ἔμελλεν αὐτὼ καλώ τε κἀγαθὼ ποιήσειν τὴν προσήκουσαν
B ἀρετήν· ἦν δ᾽ ἂν οὗτος ἢ τῶν ἱππικῶν τις ἢ τῶν γεωργικῶν· νῦν δ᾽ ἐπειδὴ ἀνθρώπω ἐστόν, τίνα αὐτοῖν ἐν νῷ ἔχεις ἐπιστάτην λαβεῖν; τίς τῆς τοιαύτης ἀρετῆς, τῆς ἀνθρωπίνης τε καὶ πολιτικῆς, ἐπιστήμων ἐστίν; οἶμαι γάρ σε ἐσκέφθαι διὰ τὴν τῶν υἱέων κτῆσιν. ἔστι τις, ἔφην ἐγώ, ἢ οὔ; Πάνυ γε, ᾗ δ᾽ ὅς. Τίς, ἦν δ᾽ ἐγώ, καὶ ποδαπός, καὶ πόσου διδάσκει; Εὔηνός, ἔφη, ὦ Σώκρατες, Πάριος, πέντε μνῶν· καὶ ἐγὼ τὸν Εὔηνον ἐμακάρισα, εἰ ὡς ἀληθῶς ἔχει
C ταύτην τὴν τέχνην καὶ οὕτως ἐμμελῶς διδάσκει. ἐγὼ οὖν καὶ αὐτὸς ἐκαλλυνόμην τε καὶ ἡβρυνόμην ἄν, εἰ ἠπιστάμην ταῦτα· ἀλλ᾽ οὐ γὰρ ἐπίσταμαι, ὦ ἄνδρες Ἀθηναῖοι.

'Then how have you got your extraordinary reputation, Socrates?'
If I am reported wise, it is owing to the response which Apollo gave to Chaerephon.

Ὑπολάβοι ἂν οὖν τις ὑμῶν ἴσως· ἀλλ᾽, ὦ Σώ- Socrates
κρατες, τὸ σὸν τί ἐστι πρᾶγμα; πόθεν αἱ διαβολαί σοι explains
how he

αὗται γεγόνασιν; οὐ γὰρ δήπου σοῦ γε οὐδὲν τῶν ἄλλων περιττότερον πραγματευομένου ἔπειτα τοσαύτη φήμη τε καὶ λόγος γέγονεν [εἰ μή τι ἔπραττες ἀλλοῖον ἢ οἱ πολλοί]· λέγε οὖν ἡμῖν, τί ἐστιν, ἵνα μὴ ἡμεῖς περὶ σοῦ αὐτοσχεδιάζωμεν. ταυτί μοι δοκεῖ δίκαια λέγειν ὁ λέγων, κἀγὼ D ὑμῖν πειράσομαι ἀποδεῖξαι, τί ποτ᾽ ἔστι τοῦτο ὃ ἐμοὶ πεποίηκε τό τε ὄνομα καὶ τὴν διαβολήν. ἀκούετε δή. καὶ ἴσως μὲν δόξω τισὶν ὑμῶν παίζειν, εὖ μέντοι ἴστε, πᾶσαν ὑμῖν τὴν ἀλήθειαν ἐρῶ. ἐγὼ γάρ, ὦ ἄνδρες Ἀθηναῖοι, δι᾽ οὐδὲν ἀλλ᾽ ἢ διὰ σοφίαν τινὰ τοῦτο τὸ ὄνομα ἔσχηκα. ποίαν δὴ σοφίαν ταύτην; ἥπερ ἐστὶν ἴσως ἀνθρωπίνη σοφία. τῷ ὄντι γὰρ κινδυνεύω ταύτην εἶναι σοφός· οὗτοι δὲ τάχ᾽ ἄν, οὓς ἄρτι ἔλεγον, μείζω τινὰ ἢ κατ᾽ ἄνθρωπον σοφίαν σοφοὶ εἶεν, ἢ οὐκ ἔχω τί λέγω· οὐ γὰρ E δὴ ἔγωγε αὐτὴν ἐπίσταμαι, ἀλλ᾽ ὅστις φησὶ ψεύδεταί τε καὶ ἐπὶ διαβολῇ τῇ ἐμῇ λέγει. καί μοι, ὦ ἄνδρες Ἀθηναῖοι, μὴ θορυβήσητε, μηδ᾽ ἐὰν δόξω τι ὑμῖν μέγα λέγειν· οὐ γὰρ ἐμὸν ἐρῶ τὸν λόγον, ὃν ἂν λέγω, ἀλλ᾽ εἰς ἀξιόχρεων ὑμῖν τὸν λέγοντα ἀνοίσω. τῆς γὰρ ἐμῆς, εἰ δή τίς ἐστι σοφία καὶ οἵα, μάρτυρα ὑμῖν παρέξομαι τὸν θεὸν τὸν ἐν Δελφοῖς. Χαιρεφῶντα γὰρ ἴστε που. οὗτος ἐμός τε ἑταῖρος ἦν ἐκ νέου, 21 καὶ ὑμῶν τῷ πλήθει ἑταῖρός τε καὶ ξυνέφυγε τὴν φυγὴν ταύτην καὶ μεθ᾽ ὑμῶν κατῆλθε. καὶ ἴστε δὴ οἷος ἦν Χαιρεφῶν, ὡς σφοδρὸς ἐφ᾽ ὅ τι ὁρμήσειε. καὶ δή ποτε καὶ εἰς Δελφοὺς ἐλθὼν ἐτόλμησε τοῦτο μαντεύσασθαι· καί, ὅπερ λέγω, μὴ θορυβεῖτε, ὦ ἄνδρες· ἤρετο γὰρ δή, εἴ τις ἐμοῦ εἴη σοφώτερος. ἀνεῖλεν οὖν ἡ Πυθία μηδένα σοφώτερον εἶναι. καὶ τούτων πέρι ὁ ἀδελφὸς ὑμῖν αὐτοῦ οὑτοσὶ μαρτυρήσει, ἐπειδὴ ἐκεῖνος τετελεύτηκεν.

When I heard the oracle from Delphi, I proceeded to test its truth by comparing myself with others. First I tried the politicians, and found that they were not aware of their own ignorance, whereas I knew mine.

B Σκέψασθε δὲ ὧν ἕνεκα ταῦτα λέγω· μέλλω γὰρ ὑμᾶς διδάξειν, ὅθεν μοι ἡ διαβολὴ γέγονε. ταῦτα γὰρ ἐγὼ ἀκούσας ἐνεθυμούμην οὑτωσί· τί ποτε λέγει ὁ θεός, καὶ τί ποτε αἰνίττεται; ἐγὼ γὰρ δὴ οὔτε μέγα οὔτε σμικρὸν ξύνοιδα ἐμαυτῷ σοφὸς ὤν· τί οὖν ποτὲ λέγει φάσκων ἐμὲ σοφώτατον εἶναι; οὐ γὰρ δήπου ψεύδεταί γε· οὐ γὰρ θέμις αὐτῷ. καὶ πολὺν μὲν χρόνον ἠπόρουν, τί ποτε λέγει, ἔπειτα μόγις πάνυ ἐπὶ ζήτησιν αὐτοῦ τοιαύτην τινὰ ἐτραπόμην. ἦλθον ἐπί τινα τῶν δοκούντων σοφῶν εἶναι, ὡς
C ἐνταῦθα, εἴ πέρ που, ἐλέγξων τὸ μαντεῖον καὶ ἀποφανῶν τῷ χρησμῷ ὅτι οὑτοσὶ ἐμοῦ σοφώτερός ἐστι, σὺ δ᾽ ἐμὲ ἔφησθα. διασκοπῶν οὖν τοῦτον—ὀνόματι γὰρ οὐδὲν δέομαι λέγειν, ἦν δέ τις τῶν πολιτικῶν, πρὸς ὃν ἐγὼ σκοπῶν τοιοῦτόν τι ἔπαθον, ὦ ἄνδρες Ἀθηναῖοι—καὶ διαλεγόμενος αὐτῷ, ἔδοξέ μοι οὗτος ὁ ἀνὴρ δοκεῖν μὲν εἶναι σοφὸς ἄλλοις τε πολλοῖς ἀνθρώποις καὶ μάλιστα ἑαυτῷ, εἶναι δ᾽ οὔ· κἄπειτα ἐπειρώμην αὐτῷ δεικνύναι, ὅτι οἴοιτο μὲν
D εἶναι σοφός, εἴη δ᾽ οὔ. ἐντεῦθεν οὖν τούτῳ τε ἀπηχθόμην καὶ πολλοῖς τῶν παρόντων, πρὸς ἐμαυτὸν δ᾽ οὖν ἀπιὼν ἐλογιζόμην ὅτι τούτου μὲν τοῦ ἀνθρώπου ἐγὼ σοφώτερός εἰμι· κινδυνεύει μὲν γὰρ ἡμῶν οὐδέτερος οὐδὲν καλὸν κἀγαθὸν εἰδέναι, ἀλλ᾽ οὗτος μὲν οἴεταί τι εἰδέναι οὐκ εἰδώς, ἐγὼ δέ, ὥσπερ οὖν οὐκ οἶδα, οὐδὲ οἴομαι· ἔοικα γοῦν τούτου γε σμικρῷ τινι αὐτῷ τούτῳ σοφώτερος εἶναι, ὅτι ἃ μὴ οἶδα οὐδὲ οἴομαι εἰδέναι. ἐντεῦθεν ἐπ᾽ ἄλλον ᾖα τῶν ἐκείνου δοκούντων σοφωτέρων εἶναι, καί μοι ταὐτὰ

Socrates tests its truth by a comparison of himself with others.

The politicians

38   *APOLOGY*, 21 E—22 C.

ταῦτα ἔδοξε· καὶ ἐνταῦθα κἀκείνῳ καὶ ἄλλοις πολλοῖς Ε
ἀπηχθόμην.

*Next I examined the poets, and found that they could give no
intelligible account of their own productions.*

Μετὰ ταῦτ' οὖν ἤδη ἐφεξῆς ᾖα, αἰσθανόμενος μὲν
καὶ λυπούμενος καὶ δεδιὼς ὅτι ἀπηχθανόμην, ὅμως δὲ
ἀναγκαῖον ἐδόκει εἶναι τὸ τοῦ θεοῦ περὶ πλείστου ποι-
εῖσθαι· ἰτέον οὖν σκοποῦντι τὸν χρησμόν, τί λέγει, ἐπὶ
ἅπαντας τοὺς τι δοκοῦντας εἰδέναι. καὶ νὴ τὸν κύνα, ὦ
ἄνδρες Ἀθηναῖοι· δεῖ γὰρ πρὸς ὑμᾶς τἀληθῆ λέγειν· ἦ 22
μὴν ἐγὼ ἔπαθόν τι τοιοῦτον· οἱ μὲν μάλιστα εὐδοκιμοῦντες
ἔδοξάν μοι ὀλίγου δεῖν τοῦ πλείστου ἐνδεεῖς εἶναι ζητοῦντι
κατὰ τὸν θεόν, ἄλλοι δὲ δοκοῦντες φαυλότεροι ἐπιεικέσ-
τεροι εἶναι ἄνδρες πρὸς τὸ φρονίμως ἔχειν. δεῖ δὴ ὑμῖν
τὴν ἐμὴν πλάνην ἐπιδεῖξαι ὥσπερ πόνους τινὰς πονοῦντος,
ἵνα μοι καὶ ἀνέλεγκτος ἡ μαντεία γένοιτο. μετὰ γὰρ τοὺς
The poets. πολιτικοὺς ᾖα ἐπὶ τοὺς ποιητὰς τούς τε τῶν τραγῳδιῶν καὶ
τοὺς τῶν διθυράμβων καὶ τοὺς ἄλλους, ὡς ἐνταῦθα ἐπ' Β
αὐτοφώρῳ καταληψόμενος ἐμαυτὸν ἀμαθέστερον ἐκείνων
ὄντα. ἀναλαμβάνων οὖν αὐτῶν τὰ ποιήματα, ἅ μοι ἐδόκει
μάλιστα πεπραγματεῦσθαι αὐτοῖς, διηρώτων ἂν αὐτοὺς τί
λέγοιεν, ἵν' ἅμα τι καὶ μανθάνοιμι παρ' αὐτῶν. αἰσχύνομαι
οὖν ὑμῖν εἰπεῖν, ὦ ἄνδρες, τἀληθῆ· ὅμως δὲ ῥητέον. ὡς
ἔπος γὰρ εἰπεῖν ὀλίγου αὐτῶν ἅπαντες οἱ παρόντες ἂν
βέλτιον ἔλεγον περὶ ὧν αὐτοὶ ἐπεποιήκεσαν. ἔγνων οὖν
καὶ περὶ τῶν ποιητῶν ἐν ὀλίγῳ τοῦτο, ὅτι οὐ σοφίᾳ
ποιοῖεν ἃ ποιοῖεν, ἀλλὰ φύσει τινὶ καὶ ἐνθουσιάζοντες, C
ὥσπερ οἱ θεομάντεις καὶ οἱ χρησμῳδοί· καὶ γὰρ οὗτοι
λέγουσι μὲν πολλὰ καὶ καλά, ἴσασι δὲ οὐδὲν ὧν λέγουσι.
τοιοῦτόν τί μοι ἐφάνησαν πάθος καὶ οἱ ποιηταὶ πεπονθότες·

καὶ ἅμα ᾐσθόμην αὐτῶν διὰ τὴν ποίησιν οἰομένων καὶ
τἆλλα σοφωτάτων εἶναι ἀνθρώπων, ἃ οὐκ ἦσαν. ἀπῇα οὖν
καὶ ἐντεῦθεν τῷ αὐτῷ οἰόμενος περιγεγονέναι, ᾧπερ καὶ
τῶν πολιτικῶν.

Lastly I went to the artisans. They undoubtedly possessed great technical skill, but this only served to inspire a conceit of their own knowledge on subjects of the deepest importance.

Τελευτῶν οὖν ἐπὶ τοὺς χειροτέχνας ᾖα· ἐμαυτῷ γὰρ The
D ξυνῄδειν οὐδὲν ἐπισταμένῳ, ὡς ἔπος εἰπεῖν, τούτους δέ   artisans.
γ' ᾔδειν ὅτι εὑρήσοιμι πολλὰ καὶ καλὰ ἐπισταμένους.
καὶ τούτου μὲν οὐκ ἐψεύσθην, ἀλλ' ἠπίσταντο ἃ ἐγὼ οὐκ
ἠπιστάμην καί μου ταύτῃ σοφώτεροι ἦσαν. ἀλλ', ὦ ἄνδρες
Ἀθηναῖοι, ταὐτόν μοι ἔδοξαν ἔχειν ἁμάρτημα, ὅπερ καὶ οἱ
ποιηταί, καὶ οἱ ἀγαθοὶ δημιουργοί· διὰ τὸ τὴν τέχνην
καλῶς ἐξεργάζεσθαι ἕκαστος ἠξίου καὶ τἆλλα τὰ μέγιστα
σοφώτατος εἶναι, καὶ αὐτῶν αὕτη ἡ πλημμέλεια ἐκείνην
E τὴν σοφίαν ἀπέκρυπτεν· ὥστ' ἐμὲ ἐμαυτὸν ἀνερωτᾶν ὑπὲρ
τοῦ χρησμοῦ, πότερα δεξαίμην ἂν οὕτως ὥσπερ ἔχω ἔχειν,
μήτε τι σοφὸς ὢν τὴν ἐκείνων σοφίαν μήτε ἀμαθὴς τὴν ἀμα-
θίαν, ἢ ἀμφότερα ἃ ἐκεῖνοι ἔχουσιν ἔχειν. ἀπεκρινάμην οὖν
ἐμαυτῷ καὶ τῷ χρησμῷ, ὅτι μοι λυσιτελοῖ ὥσπερ ἔχω ἔχειν.

These inquiries have led to many enmities, and plunged me in poverty, as I have had no time to attend to my private affairs.

Ἐκ ταυτησὶ δὴ τῆς ἐξετάσεως, ὦ ἄνδρες Ἀθηναῖοι, Conse-
                                                                                quences of
23 πολλαὶ μὲν ἀπέχθειαί μοι γεγόνασι καὶ οἷαι χαλεπώταται these
καὶ βαρύταται, ὥστε πολλὰς διαβολὰς ἀπ' αὐτῶν γεγονέ-   inquiries.
ναι, ὄνομα δὲ τοῦτο λέγεσθαι, σοφὸς εἶναι. οἴονται γάρ με
ἑκάστοτε οἱ παρόντες ταῦτα αὐτὸν εἶναι σοφόν, ἃ ἂν
ἄλλον ἐξελέγξω· τὸ δὲ κινδυνεύει, ὦ ἄνδρες, τῷ ὄντι ὁ

θεὸς σοφὸς εἶναι, καὶ ἐν τῷ χρησμῷ τούτῳ τοῦτο λέγειν, ὅτι ἡ ἀνθρωπίνη σοφία ὀλίγου τινὸς ἀξία ἐστὶ καὶ οὐδενός· καὶ φαίνεται τοῦτ' οὐ λέγειν τὸν Σωκράτη, προσκεχρῆσθαι δὲ τῷ ἐμῷ ὀνόματι, ἐμὲ παράδειγμα ποιούμενος, ὥσπερ ἂν εἰ εἴποι ὅτι οὗτος ὑμῶν, ὦ ἄνθρωποι, σοφώτατός ἐστιν, B ὅστις ὥσπερ Σωκράτης ἔγνωκεν ὅτι οὐδενὸς ἄξιός ἐστι τῇ ἀληθείᾳ πρὸς σοφίαν. ταῦτ' οὖν ἐγὼ μὲν ἔτι καὶ νῦν περιιὼν ζητῶ καὶ ἐρευνῶ κατὰ τὸν θεόν, καὶ τῶν ἀστῶν καὶ τῶν ξένων ἄν τινα οἴωμαι σοφὸν εἶναι· καὶ ἐπειδάν μοι μὴ δοκῇ, τῷ θεῷ βοηθῶν ἐνδείκνυμαι ὅτι οὐκ ἔστι σοφός. καὶ ὑπὸ ταύτης τῆς ἀσχολίας οὔτε τι τῶν τῆς πόλεως πρᾶξαί μοι σχολὴ γέγονεν ἄξιον λόγου οὔτε τῶν οἰκείων, ἀλλ' ἐν πενίᾳ μυρίᾳ εἰμὶ διὰ τὴν τοῦ θεοῦ λατρείαν.

Moreover the young men took delight in hearing my cross-examination of those who pretended to knowledge, and began to imitate me themselves. Hence their victims in a blind rage levelled at me the charges which are brought against all philosophers. These are the real grounds for the present prosecution.

Exasperation caused by the young men imitating Socrates.

Πρὸς δὲ τούτοις οἱ νέοι μοι ἐπακολουθοῦντες, οἷς C μάλιστα σχολή ἐστιν, οἱ τῶν πλουσιωτάτων, αὐτόματοι χαίρουσιν ἀκούοντες ἐξεταζομένων τῶν ἀνθρώπων, καὶ αὐτοὶ πολλάκις ἐμὲ μιμοῦνται, εἶτ' ἐπιχειροῦσιν ἄλλους ἐξετάζειν· κἄπειτα, οἶμαι, εὑρίσκουσι πολλὴν ἀφθονίαν οἰομένων μὲν εἰδέναι τι ἀνθρώπων, εἰδότων δὲ ὀλίγα ἢ οὐδέν. ἐντεῦθεν οὖν οἱ ὑπ' αὐτῶν ἐξεταζόμενοι ἐμοὶ ὀργίζονται, ἀλλ' οὐχ αὑτοῖς, καὶ λέγουσιν ὡς Σωκράτης τίς ἐστι μιαρώτατος καὶ διαφθείρει τοὺς νέους· καὶ ἐπει- D δάν τις αὐτοὺς ἐρωτᾷ, ὅ τι ποιῶν καὶ ὅ τι διδάσκων, ἔχουσι μὲν οὐδὲν εἰπεῖν, ἀλλ' ἀγνοοῦσιν, ἵνα δὲ μὴ δοκῶσιν ἀπορεῖν, τὰ κατὰ πάντων τῶν φιλοσοφούντων πρόχεῖρα ταῦτα λέγουσιν, ὅτι τὰ μετέωρα καὶ τὰ ὑπὸ γῆς, καὶ θεοὺς μὴ νομίζειν, καὶ τὸν ἥττω λόγον κρείττω ποιεῖν. τὰ γὰρ ἀληθῆ, οἶμαι, οὐκ ἂν ἐθέλοιεν λέγειν, ὅτι κατάδηλοι γίγνονται προσποιούμενοι μὲν εἰδέναι, εἰδότες δὲ οὐδέν. ἅτε οὖν, οἶμαι, φιλότιμοι ὄντες καὶ σφοδροὶ καὶ πολλοί, E καὶ ξυντεταγμένως καὶ πιθανῶς λέγοντες περὶ ἐμοῦ, ἐμπεπλήκασιν ὑμῶν τὰ ὦτα καὶ πάλαι καὶ σφοδρῶς διαβάλλοντες. ἐκ τούτων καὶ Μέλητός μοι ἐπέθετο καὶ Ἄνυτος καὶ Λύκων, Μέλητος μὲν ὑπὲρ τῶν ποιητῶν ἀχθόμενος, Ἄνυτος δὲ ὑπὲρ τῶν δημιουργῶν καὶ τῶν πολιτικῶν, 24 Λύκων δὲ ὑπὲρ τῶν ῥητόρων· ὥστε, ὅπερ ἀρχόμενος ἐγὼ ἔλεγον, θαυμάζοιμ᾽ ἂν εἰ οἷός τ᾽ εἴην ἐγὼ ὑμῶν ταύτην τὴν διαβολὴν ἐξελέσθαι ἐν οὕτως ὀλίγῳ χρόνῳ οὕτω πολλὴν γεγονυῖαν. ταῦτ᾽ ἔστιν ὑμῖν, ὦ ἄνδρες Ἀθηναῖοι, τἀληθῆ, καὶ ὑμᾶς οὔτε μέγα οὔτε σμικρὸν ἀποκρυψάμενος ἐγὼ λέγω οὐδ᾽ ὑποστειλάμενος. καί τοι οἶδα σχεδὸν ὅτι τοῖς αὐτοῖς ἀπεχθάνομαι· ὃ καὶ τεκμήριον ὅτι ἀληθῆ λέγω B καὶ ὅτι αὕτη ἐστὶν ἡ διαβολὴ ἡ ἐμὴ καὶ τὰ αἴτια ταῦτά ἐστι. καὶ ἐάν τε νῦν ἐάν τε αὖθις ζητήσητε ταῦτα, οὕτως εὑρήσετε.

Interests represented by the three accusers severally.

(b) **Defence against the specific indictment, 24 B-28 A.**

It is now time to turn to Meletus and his indictment. He is guilty of trifling on a serious matter.

Περὶ μὲν οὖν ὧν οἱ πρῶτοί μου κατήγοροι κατηγόρουν αὕτη ἔστω ἱκανὴ ἀπολογία πρὸς ὑμᾶς· πρὸς δὲ Μέλητον τὸν ἀγαθόν τε καὶ φιλόπολιν, ὥς φησι, καὶ τοὺς ὑστέρους μετὰ ταῦτα πειράσομαι ἀπολογεῖσθαι. αὖθις γὰρ δή, ὥσπερ ἑτέρων τούτων ὄντων κατηγόρων, λάβωμεν αὖ τὴν τούτων ἀντωμοσίαν. ἔχει δέ πως ὧδε· Σωκράτη φησὶν ἀδικεῖν τούς τε νέους διαφθείροντα καὶ θεοὺς οὓς ἡ πόλις νομίζει οὐ νομίζοντα, ἕτερα δὲ δαι-

The accusation formulated.
(1) Perversion of the youth.
(2) Atheism

μόνια καινά. τὸ μὲν δὴ ἔγκλημα τοιοῦτόν ἐστι· τούτου C
δὲ τοῦ ἐγκλήματος ἓν ἕκαστον ἐξετάσωμεν. φησὶ γὰρ

Its want of seriousness. δὴ τοὺς νέους ἀδικεῖν με διαφθείροντα. ἐγὼ δέ γε, ὦ ἄνδρες Ἀθηναῖοι, ἀδικεῖν φημὶ Μέλητον, ὅτι σπουδῇ χαριεντίζεται, ῥᾳδίως εἰς ἀγῶνας καθιστὰς ἀνθρώπους, περὶ πραγμάτων προσποιούμενος σπουδάζειν καὶ κήδεσθαι, ὧν οὐδὲν τούτῳ πώποτε ἐμέλησεν. ὡς δὲ τοῦτο οὕτως ἔχει, πειράσομαι καὶ ὑμῖν ἐπιδεῖξαι.

You profess a care for the youth, Meletus, and say that I corrupt them. Who then improves them? 'The jurors, audience, everyone.' Then I alone corrupt them! But that is absurd.

Ἡ ἐρώτησις.
24 C-28 A.

(1) Charge of perverting the youth met, 24 C-26 A.

Καί μοι δεῦρο, ὦ Μέλητε, εἰπέ· ἄλλο τι ἢ περὶ πολλοῦ ποιεῖ, ὅπως ὡς βέλτιστοι οἱ νεώτεροι ἔσονται; D Ἔγωγε. Ἴθι δὴ νῦν εἰπὲ τούτοις, τίς αὐτοὺς βελτίους ποιεῖ; δῆλον γὰρ ὅτι οἶσθα, μέλον γέ σοι. τὸν μὲν γὰρ διαφθείροντα ἐξευρών, ὡς φῄς, ἐμὲ εἰσάγεις τουτοισὶ καὶ κατηγορεῖς· τὸν δὲ δὴ βελτίους ποιοῦντα ἴθι εἰπὲ καὶ μήνυσον αὐτοῖς, τίς ἐστιν. ὁρᾷς, ὦ Μέλητε, ὅτι σιγᾷς καὶ οὐκ ἔχεις εἰπεῖν; καί τοι οὐκ αἰσχρόν σοι δοκεῖ εἶναι καὶ ἱκανὸν τεκμήριον οὗ δὴ ἐγὼ λέγω, ὅτι σοι οὐδὲν μεμέληκεν; ἀλλ' εἰπέ, ὦ 'γαθέ, τίς αὐτοὺς ἀμείνους ποιεῖ; Οἱ νόμοι. Ἀλλ' οὐ τοῦτο ἐρωτῶ, ὦ E βέλτιστε, ἀλλὰ τίς ἄνθρωπος, ὅστις πρῶτον καὶ αὐτὸ τοῦτο οἶδε, τοὺς νόμους. Οὗτοι, ὦ Σώκρατες, οἱ δικασταί. Πῶς λέγεις, ὦ Μέλητε; οἵδε τοὺς νέους παιδεύειν οἷοί τέ εἰσι καὶ βελτίους ποιεῖν; Μάλιστα. Πότερον ἅπαντες, ἢ οἱ μὲν αὐτῶν, οἱ δ' οὔ; Ἅπαντες. Εὖ γε νὴ τὴν Ἥραν λέγεις, καὶ πολλὴν ἀφθονίαν τῶν ὠφελούντων. τί δὲ δή; οἵδε οἱ ἀκροαταὶ βελτίους ποιοῦσιν, 25 ἢ οὔ; Καὶ οὗτοι. Τί δὲ οἱ βουλευταί; Καὶ οἱ βουλευ-

ταί. Ἀλλ' ἄρα, ὦ Μέλητε, μὴ οἱ ἐν τῇ ἐκκλησίᾳ, [οἱ ἐκκλησιασταί,] διαφθείρουσι τοὺς νεωτέρους; ἢ κἀκεῖνοι βελτίους ποιοῦσιν ἅπαντες; Κἀκεῖνοι. Πάντες ἄρα, ὡς ἔοικεν, Ἀθηναῖοι καλοὺς κἀγαθοὺς ποιοῦσι πλὴν ἐμοῦ, ἐγὼ δὲ μόνος διαφθείρω. οὕτω λέγεις; Πάνυ σφόδρα ταῦτα λέγω Πολλήν γ' ἐμοῦ κατέγνωκας δυστυχίαν. καί μοι ἀπόκριναι· ἦ καὶ περὶ ἵππους οὕτω σοι δοκεῖ
B ἔχειν· οἱ μὲν βελτίους ποιοῦντες αὐτοὺς πάντες ἄνθρωποι εἶναι, εἷς δέ τις ὁ διαφθείρων; ἢ τοὐναντίον τούτου πᾶν εἷς μέν τις ὁ βελτίους οἷός τ' ὢν ποιεῖν ἢ πάνυ ὀλίγοι, οἱ ἱππικοί· οἱ δὲ πολλοὶ ἐάνπερ ξυνῶσι καὶ χρῶνται ἵπποις, διαφθείρουσιν; οὐχ οὕτως ἔχει, ὦ Μέλητε, καὶ περὶ ἵππων καὶ τῶν ἄλλων ἁπάντων ζῴων; πάντως δήπου, ἐάν τε σὺ καὶ Ἄνυτος οὐ φῆτε ἐάν τε φῆτε· πολλὴ γὰρ ἂν τις εὐδαιμονία εἴη περὶ τοὺς νέους, εἰ εἷς μὲν μόνος αὐτοὺς διαφθείρει, οἱ δ' ἄλλοι ὠφελοῦσιν.
C ἀλλὰ γάρ, ὦ Μέλητε, ἱκανῶς ἐπιδείκνυσαι ὅτι οὐδεπώποτε ἐφρόντισας τῶν νέων, καὶ σαφῶς ἀποφαίνεις τὴν σαυτοῦ ἀμέλειαν, ὅτι οὐδέν σοι μεμέληκε περὶ ὧν ἐμὲ εἰσάγεις.

Again, am I so foolish, Meletus, as to wish to live among bad fellow-citizens? No! The harm that I do must be involuntary. And why bring me to trial for an involuntary act?

Ἔτι δὲ ἡμῖν εἰπέ, ὦ πρὸς Διός, Μέλητε, πότερον ἐστιν οἰκεῖν ἄμεινον ἐν πολίταις χρηστοῖς ἢ πονηροῖς; ὦ 'τᾶν, ἀπόκριναι· οὐδὲν γάρ τοι χαλεπὸν ἐρωτῶ. οὐχ οἱ μὲν πονηροὶ κακόν τι ἐργάζονται τοὺς ἀεὶ ἐγγυτάτω ἑαυτῶν ὄντας, οἱ δ' ἀγαθοὶ ἀγαθόν τι; Πάνυ γε. Ἔστιν οὖν ὅστις βούλεται ὑπὸ τῶν ξυνόντων
D βλάπτεσθαι μᾶλλον ἢ ὠφελεῖσθαι; ἀπόκριναι, ὦ 'γαθέ·

καὶ γὰρ ὁ νόμος κελεύει ἀποκρίνεσθαι. ἔσθ' ὅστις βούλεται βλάπτεσθαι; Οὐ δῆτα. Φέρε δή, πότερον ἐμὲ εἰσάγεις δεῦρο ὡς διαφθείροντα τοὺς νεωτέρους καὶ πονηροτέρους ποιοῦντα ἑκόντα ἢ ἄκοντα; Ἑκόντα ἔγωγε. Τί δῆτα, ὦ Μέλητε; τοσοῦτον σὺ ἐμοῦ σοφώτερος εἶ τηλικούτου ὄντος τηλικόσδε ὤν, ὥστε σὺ μὲν ἔγνωκας ὅτι οἱ μὲν κακοὶ κακόν τι ἐργάζονται ἀεὶ τοὺς μάλιστα πλησίον ἑαυτῶν, οἱ δὲ ἀγαθοὶ ἀγαθόν· ἐγὼ δὲ δὴ εἰς Ε τοσοῦτον ἀμαθίας ἥκω, ὥστε καὶ τοῦτ' ἀγνοῶ, ὅτι, ἐάν τινα μοχθηρὸν ποιήσω τῶν ξυνόντων, κινδυνεύσω κακόν τι λαβεῖν ὑπ' αὐτοῦ, ὥστε τοῦτο τὸ τοσοῦτον κακὸν ἑκὼν ποιῶ, ὡς φῂς σύ; ταῦτα ἐγώ σοι οὐ πείθομαι, ὦ Μέλητε, οἶμαι δὲ οὐδὲ ἄλλον ἀνθρώπων οὐδένα· ἀλλ' 26 ἢ οὐ διαφθείρω, ἢ εἰ διαφθείρω, ἄκων, ὥστε σύ γε κατ' ἀμφότερα ψεύδει. εἰ δὲ ἄκων διαφθείρω, τῶν τοιούτων [καὶ ἀκουσίων] ἁμαρτημάτων οὐ δεῦρο νόμος εἰσάγειν ἐστίν, ἀλλ' ἰδίᾳ λαβόντα διδάσκειν καὶ νουθετεῖν· δῆλον γὰρ ὅτι, ἐὰν μάθω, παύσομαι ὅ γε ἄκων ποιῶ. σὺ δὲ ξυγγενέσθαι μέν μοι καὶ διδάξαι ἔφυγες καὶ οὐκ ἠθέλησας, δεῦρο δὲ εἰσάγεις, οἷ νόμος ἐστὶν εἰσάγειν τοὺς κολάσεως δεομένους, ἀλλ' οὐ μαθήσεως.

'You are an atheist, Socrates. You say that the sun is a stone, and the moon earth.' As if everyone did not know that these are the doctrines of Anaxagoras, not mine! The accusation is not only false, but self-contradictory.

(2) Charge of atheism met, 26 A.-28 A.

Ἀλλὰ γάρ, ὦ ἄνδρες Ἀθηναῖοι, τοῦτο μὲν δῆλον ἤδη ἐστίν, ὃ ἐγὼ ἔλεγον, ὅτι Μελήτῳ τούτων οὔτε μέγα οὔτε Β σμικρὸν πώποτε ἐμέλησεν· ὅμως δὲ δὴ λέγε ἡμῖν, πῶς με φῂς διαφθείρειν, ὦ Μέλητε, τοὺς νεωτέρους; ἢ δῆλον δὴ ὅτι κατὰ τὴν γραφήν, ἣν ἐγράψω, θεοὺς διδάσκοντα μὴ νομίζειν οὓς ἡ πόλις νομίζει, ἕτερα δὲ δαιμόνια καινά; οὐ

ταῦτα λέγεις ὅτι διδάσκων διαφθείρω; Πάνυ μὲν οὖν σφόδρα ταῦτα λέγω. Πρὸς αὐτῶν τοίνυν, ὦ Μέλητε, τούτων τῶν θεῶν, ὧν νῦν ὁ λόγος ἐστίν, εἰπὲ ἔτι σαφέ-
C στερον καὶ ἐμοὶ καὶ τοῖς ἀνδράσι τουτοισί. ἐγὼ γὰρ οὐ δύναμαι μαθεῖν, πότερον λέγεις διδάσκειν με νομίζειν εἶναί τινας θεούς, καὶ αὐτὸς ἄρα νομίζω εἶναι θεούς, καὶ οὐκ εἰμὶ τὸ παράπαν ἄθεος οὐδὲ ταύτῃ ἀδικῶ, οὐ μέντοι οὕσπερ γε ἡ πόλις, ἀλλ' ἑτέρους, καὶ τοῦτ' ἔστιν ὅ μοι ἐγκαλεῖς, ὅτι ἑτέρους· ἢ παντάπασί με φῂς οὔτε αὐτὸν νομίζειν θεοὺς τούς τε ἄλλους ταῦτα διδάσκειν. Ταῦτα λέγω, ὡς τὸ παράπαν οὐ νομίζεις θεούς. Ὦ θαυμάσιε
D Μέλητε, ἵνα τί ταῦτα λέγεις; οὐδὲ ἥλιον οὐδὲ σελήνην ἄρα νομίζω θεοὺς εἶναι, ὥσπερ οἱ ἄλλοι ἄνθρωποι; Μὰ Δί', ὦ ἄνδρες δικασταί, ἐπεὶ τὸν μὲν ἥλιον λίθον φησὶν εἶναι, τὴν δὲ σελήνην γῆν. Ἀναξαγόρου οἴει κατηγορεῖν, ὦ φίλε Μέλητε, καὶ οὕτω καταφρονεῖς τῶνδε καὶ οἴει αὐτοὺς ἀπείρους γραμμάτων εἶναι, ὥστε οὐκ εἰδέναι ὅτι τὰ Ἀναξαγόρου βιβλία τοῦ Κλαζομενίου γέμει τούτων τῶν λόγων; καὶ δὴ καὶ οἱ νέοι ταῦτα παρ' ἐμοῦ μανθάνουσιν,
E ἃ ἔξεστιν ἐνίοτε, εἰ πάνυ πολλοῦ, δραχμῆς ἐκ τῆς ὀρχήστρας πριαμένοις Σωκράτους καταγελᾶν, ἐὰν προσποιῆται ἑαυτοῦ εἶναι, ἄλλως τε καὶ οὕτως ἄτοπα ὄντα. ἀλλ' ὦ πρὸς Διός, οὑτωσί σοι δοκῶ οὐδένα νομίζειν θεὸν εἶναι; Οὐ μέντοι μὰ Δί', οὐδ' ὁπωστιοῦν. Ἄπιστός γ' εἶ, ὦ Μέλητε, καὶ ταῦτα μέντοι, ὡς ἐμοὶ δοκεῖς, σαυτῷ. ἐμοὶ μὲν γὰρ δοκεῖ οὑτοσί, ὦ ἄνδρες Ἀθηναῖοι, πάνυ εἶναι ὑβριστὴς καὶ ἀκόλαστος, καὶ ἀτεχνῶς τὴν γραφὴν ταύτην ὕβρει τινὶ καὶ ἀκολασίᾳ
27 καὶ νεότητι γράψασθαι. ἔοικε γὰρ ὥσπερ αἴνιγμα ξυντιθέντι διαπειρωμένῳ, ἆρα γνώσεται Σωκράτης ὁ σοφὸς δὴ ἐμοῦ χαριεντιζομένου καὶ ἐναντί' ἐμαυτῷ λέγοντος, ἢ ἐξαπατήσω αὐτὸν καὶ τοὺς ἄλλους τοὺς ἀκούοντας; οὗτος γὰρ ἐμοὶ

φαίνεται τὰ ἐναντία λέγειν αὐτὸς ἑαυτῷ ἐν τῇ γραφῇ, ὥσπερ ἂν εἰ εἴποι· ἀδικεῖ Σωκράτης θεοὺς οὐ νομίζων, ἀλλὰ θεοὺς νομίζων. καί τοι τοῦτό ἐστι παίζοντος.

For Meletus allows that I believe in δαιμόνια. Therefore I believe in δαίμονες; and, if in δαίμονες, then in θεοί. Thus Meletus is convicted out of his own mouth.

Ξυνεπισκέψασθε δή, ὦ ἄνδρες, ᾗ μοι φαίνεται ταῦτα λέγειν· σὺ δὲ ἡμῖν ἀπόκριναι, ὦ Μέλητε· ὑμεῖς δέ, ὅπερ B κατ' ἀρχὰς ὑμᾶς παρῃτησάμην, μέμνησθέ μοι μὴ θορυβεῖν, ἐὰν ἐν τῷ εἰωθότι τρόπῳ τοὺς λόγους ποιῶμαι. ἔστιν ὅστις ἀνθρώπων, ὦ Μέλητε, ἀνθρώπεια μὲν νομίζει πράγματ' εἶναι, ἀνθρώπους δὲ οὐ νομίζει; ἀποκρινέσθω, ὦ ἄνδρες, καὶ μὴ ἄλλα καὶ ἄλλα θορυβείτω· ἔσθ' ὅστις ἵππους μὲν οὐ νομίζει ἱππικὰ δὲ πράγματα; ἢ αὐλητὰς μὲν οὐ νομίζει, αὐλητικὰ δὲ πράγματα: οὐκ ἔστιν, ὦ ἄριστε ἀνδρῶν· εἰ μὴ σὺ βούλει ἀποκρίνασθαι, ἐγὼ σοὶ λέγω καὶ τοῖς ἄλλοις τουτοισί. ἀλλὰ τὸ ἐπὶ τούτῳ γε ἀπόκριναι· ἔσθ' ὅστις δαιμόνια μὲν νομίζει πράγματ' C εἶναι, δαίμονας δὲ οὐ νομίζει; Οὐκ ἔστιν. Ὡς ὤνησας, ὅτι μόγις ἀπεκρίνω ὑπὸ τουτωνὶ ἀναγκαζόμενος. οὐκοῦν δαιμόνια μὲν φῄς με καὶ νομίζειν καὶ διδάσκειν, εἴτ' οὖν καινὰ εἴτε παλαιά· ἀλλ' οὖν δαιμόνιά γε νομίζω κατὰ τὸν σὸν λόγον, καὶ ταῦτα καὶ διωμόσω ἐν τῇ ἀντιγραφῇ. εἰ δὲ δαιμόνια νομίζω, καὶ δαίμονας δήπου πολλὴ ἀνάγκη νομίζειν μέ ἐστιν· οὐχ οὕτως ἔχει; ἔχει δή· τίθημι γάρ σε ὁμολογοῦντα, ἐπειδὴ οὐκ ἀποκρίνει. τοὺς δὲ δαίμονας D οὐχὶ ἤτοι θεούς γε ἡγούμεθα ἢ θεῶν παῖδας; φῂς ἢ οὔ; Πάνυ γε. Οὐκοῦν εἴπερ δαίμονας ἡγοῦμαι, ὡς σὺ φῄς, εἰ μὲν θεοί τινές εἰσιν οἱ δαίμονες, τοῦτ' ἂν εἴη ὃ ἐγώ φημί σε αἰνίττεσθαι καὶ χαριεντίζεσθαι, θεοὺς οὐχ ἡγούμενον

φάναι ἐμὲ θεοὺς αὖ ἡγεῖσθαι πάλιν, ἐπειδήπερ γε δαίμονας
ἡγοῦμαι· εἰ δ' αὖ οἱ δαίμονες θεῶν παῖδές εἰσι νόθοι τινὲς
ἢ ἐκ νυμφῶν ἢ ἔκ τινων ἄλλων, ὧν δὴ καὶ λέγονται, τίς ἂν
ἀνθρώπων θεῶν μὲν παῖδας ἡγοῖτο εἶναι, θεοὺς δὲ μή;
ὁμοίως γὰρ ἂν ἄτοπον εἴη, ὥσπερ ἂν εἴ τις ἵππων μὲν
E παῖδας ἡγοῖτο ἢ καὶ ὄνων [τοὺς ἡμιόνους], ἵππους δὲ καὶ
ὄνους μὴ ἡγοῖτο εἶναι. ἀλλ', ὦ Μέλητε, οὐκ ἔστιν ὅπως
σὺ ταῦτα οὐχὶ ἀποπειρώμενος ἡμῶν ἐγράψω [τὴν γραφὴν
ταύτην], ἢ ἀπορῶν ὅ τι ἐγκαλοῖς ἐμοὶ ἀληθὲς ἀδίκημα·
ὅπως δὲ σύ τινα πείθοις ἂν καὶ σμικρὸν νοῦν ἔχοντα
ἀνθρώπων, ὡς οὐ τοῦ αὐτοῦ ἐστὶ καὶ δαιμόνια καὶ θεῖα
ἡγεῖσθαι, καὶ αὖ τοῦ αὐτοῦ μήτε δαίμονας μήτε θεοὺς μήτε
28 ἥρωας, οὐδεμία μηχανή ἐστιν.

4. The Digression—A defence by Socrates of his life generally, 28 A–34 B.

This is enough in reply to Meletus. It is not his accusation I have to fear, but the force of popular prejudice.

Ἀλλὰ γάρ, ὦ ἄνδρες Ἀθηναῖοι, ὡς μὲν ἐγὼ οὐκ ἀδικῶ
κατὰ τὴν Μελήτου γραφήν, οὐ πολλῆς μοι δοκεῖ εἶναι
ἀπολογίας, ἀλλ' ἱκανὰ καὶ ταῦτα· ὃ δὲ καὶ ἐν τοῖς ἔμ-
προσθεν ἔλεγον, ὅτι πολλή μοι ἀπέχθεια γέγονε καὶ πρὸς
πολλούς, εὖ ἴστε ὅτι ἀληθές ἐστι. καὶ τοῦτ' ἔστιν ὃ
ἐμὲ αἱρήσει, ἐάνπερ αἱρῇ, οὐ Μέλητος οὐδὲ Ἄνυτος, ἀλλ'
ἡ τῶν πολλῶν διαβολή τε καὶ φθόνος. ἃ δὴ πολλοὺς καὶ
B ἄλλους καὶ ἀγαθοὺς ἄνδρας ᾕρηκεν, οἶμαι δὲ καὶ αἱρήσειν·
οὐδὲν δὲ δεινὸν μὴ ἐν ἐμοὶ στῇ.

But I may be asked—'Is it not a disgrace, Socrates, to have acted in such a way that you are in danger of death?' No. A man's first object should not be to secure his life, but to do his duty.

Ἴσως δ' ἂν οὖν εἴποι τις· εἶτ' οὐκ αἰσχύνει, ὦ Σώκρατες, τοιοῦτον ἐπιτήδευμα ἐπιτηδεύσας, ἐξ οὗ κινδυνεύεις

νυνὶ ἀποθανεῖν; ἐγὼ δὲ τούτῳ ἂν δίκαιον λόγον ἀντείποιμι, ὅτι οὐ καλῶς λέγεις, ὦ ἄνθρωπε, εἰ οἴει δεῖν κίνδυνον ὑπολογίζεσθαι τοῦ ζῆν ἢ τεθνάναι ἄνδρα ὅτου τι καὶ σμικρὸν ὄφελός ἐστιν, ἀλλ' οὐκ ἐκεῖνο μόνον σκοπεῖν, ὅταν πράττῃ, πότερον δίκαια ἢ ἄδικα πράττει, καὶ ἀνδρὸς ἀγαθοῦ ἔργα ἢ κακοῦ. φαῦλοι γὰρ ἂν τῷ γε σῷ λόγῳ εἶεν τῶν ἡμιθέων ὅσοι ἐν Τροίᾳ τετελευτήκασιν, οἵ τε ἄλλοι C

Example of Achilles. καὶ ὁ τῆς Θέτιδος υἱός, ὃς τοσοῦτον τοῦ κινδύνου κατεφρόνησε παρὰ τὸ αἰσχρόν τι ὑπομεῖναι. ὥστε ἐπειδὴ εἶπεν ἡ μήτηρ αὐτῷ προθυμουμένῳ Ἕκτορα ἀποκτεῖναι, θεὸς οὖσα, οὑτωσί πως, ὡς ἐγῷμαι· ὦ παῖ, εἰ τιμωρήσεις Πατρόκλῳ τῷ ἑταίρῳ τὸν φόνον καὶ Ἕκτορα ἀποκτενεῖς, αὐτὸς ἀποθανεῖ· αὐτίκα γάρ τοι, φησί, μεθ' Ἕκτορα πότμος ἑτοῖμος· ὁ δὲ ταῦτ' ἀκούσας τοῦ μὲν θανάτου καὶ τοῦ κινδύνου ὠλιγώρησε, πολὺ δὲ μᾶλλον δείσας τὸ ζῆν κακὸς ὢν καὶ τοῖς φίλοις μὴ τιμωρεῖν, αὐτίκα, φησί, D τεθναίην δίκην-ἐπιθεὶς τῷ ἀδικοῦντι, ἵνα μὴ ἐνθάδε μένω καταγέλαστος παρὰ νηυσὶ κορωνίσιν ἄχθος ἀρούρης. μὴ αὐτὸν οἴει φροντίσαι θανάτου καὶ κινδύνου; οὕτω γὰρ ἔχει, ὦ ἄνδρες Ἀθηναῖοι, τῇ ἀληθείᾳ· οὗ ἄν τις ἑαυτὸν τάξῃ [ἢ] ἡγησάμενος βέλτιστον εἶναι ἢ ὑπ' ἄρχοντος ταχθῇ, ἐνταῦθα δεῖ, ὡς ἐμοὶ δοκεῖ, μένοντα κινδυνεύειν, μηδὲν ὑπολογιζόμενον μήτε θάνατον μήτε ἄλλο μηδὲν πρὸ τοῦ αἰσχροῦ.

I have kept my post under earthly commanders; I will keep it under the heavenly. For to dread death more than disloyalty is to assume a knowledge which we do not possess. So that if you were to offer me my life now on condition of my abandoning philosophy, I would refuse with all respect. Nay, as long as I had any breath in my body, I would continue my mission to young and old.

Ἐγὼ οὖν δεινὰ ἂν εἴην εἰργασμένος, ὦ ἄνδρες Ἀθη-

Ε ναῖοι, εἰ, ὅτε μέν με οἱ ἄρχοντες ἔταττον, οὓς ὑμεῖς
εἵλεσθε ἄρχειν μου, καὶ ἐν Ποτιδαίᾳ καὶ ἐν Ἀμφιπόλει *The campaigns of Socrates.*
καὶ ἐπὶ Δηλίῳ, τότε μὲν οὗ ἐκεῖνοι ἔταττον ἔμενον ὥσπερ
καὶ ἄλλος τις καὶ ἐκινδύνευον ἀποθανεῖν, τοῦ δὲ θεοῦ
τάττοντος, ὡς ἐγὼ ᾠήθην τε καὶ ὑπέλαβον, φιλοσοφοῦντά
με δεῖν ζῆν καὶ ἐξετάζοντα ἐμαυτὸν καὶ τοὺς ἄλλους,
29 ἐνταῦθα δὲ φοβηθεὶς ἢ θάνατον ἢ ἄλλο ὁτιοῦν πρᾶγμα
λίποιμι τὴν τάξιν. δεινὸν μέντ' ἂν εἴη, καὶ ὡς ἀληθῶς τότ'
ἄν με δικαίως εἰσάγοι τις εἰς δικαστήριον, ὅτι οὐ νομίζω
θεοὺς εἶναι ἀπειθῶν τῇ μαντείᾳ καὶ δεδιὼς θάνατον καὶ
οἰόμενος σοφὸς εἶναι οὐκ ὤν. τὸ γάρ τοι θάνατον δεδιέναι,
ὦ ἄνδρες, οὐδὲν ἄλλο ἐστὶν ἢ δοκεῖν σοφὸν εἶναι μὴ ὄντα·
δοκεῖν γὰρ εἰδέναι ἐστὶν ἃ οὐκ οἶδεν. οἶδε μὲν γὰρ οὐδεὶς
τὸν θάνατον οὐδ' εἰ τυγχάνει τῷ ἀνθρώπῳ πάντων μέγιστον
ὂν τῶν ἀγαθῶν, δεδίασι δ' ὡς εὖ εἰδότες ὅτι μέγιστον
Β τῶν κακῶν ἐστί. καὶ τοῦτο πῶς οὐκ ἀμαθία ἐστὶν αὕτη ἡ
ἐπονείδιστος, ἡ τοῦ οἴεσθαι εἰδέναι ἃ οὐκ οἶδεν; ἐγὼ δέ,
ὦ ἄνδρες, τούτῳ καὶ ἐνταῦθα ἴσως διαφέρω τῶν πολλῶν
ἀνθρώπων, καὶ εἰ δή τῳ σοφώτερός του φαίην εἶναι, τούτῳ
ἄν, ὅτι οὐκ εἰδὼς ἱκανῶς περὶ τῶν ἐν Ἅιδου οὕτω καὶ
οἴομαι οὐκ εἰδέναι· τὸ δὲ ἀδικεῖν καὶ ἀπειθεῖν τῷ βελτίονι,
καὶ θεῷ καὶ ἀνθρώπῳ, ὅτι κακὸν καὶ αἰσχρόν ἐστιν οἶδα.
πρὸ οὖν τῶν κακῶν, ὧν οἶδα ὅτι κακά ἐστιν, ἃ μὴ οἶδα εἰ
ἀγαθὰ ὄντα τυγχάνει, οὐδέποτε φοβήσομαι οὐδὲ φεύξομαι·
C ὥστε οὐδ' εἴ με νῦν ὑμεῖς ἀφίετε Ἀνύτῳ ἀπιστήσαντες, ὃς
ἔφη ἢ τὴν ἀρχὴν οὐ δεῖν ἐμὲ δεῦρο εἰσελθεῖν ἤ, ἐπειδὴ
εἰσῆλθον, οὐχ οἷόν τε εἶναι τὸ μὴ ἀποκτεῖναί με, λέγων
πρὸς ὑμᾶς ὡς, εἰ διαφευξοίμην, ἤδη ἂν ὑμῶν οἱ υἱεῖς
ἐπιτηδεύοντες ἃ Σωκράτης διδάσκει πάντες παντάπασι
διαφθαρήσονται, — εἴ μοι πρὸς ταῦτα εἴποιτε· ὦ Σώκρατες, νῦν μὲν Ἀνύτῳ οὐ πεισόμεθα, ἀλλ' ἀφίεμέν σε, ἐπὶ
D

τούτῳ μέντοι, ἐφ' ᾧτε μηκέτι ἐν ταύτῃ τῇ ζητήσει διατρίβειν μηδὲ φιλοσοφεῖν· ἐὰν δὲ ἁλῷς ἔτι τοῦτο πράττων,
ἀποθανεῖ· εἰ οὖν με, ὅπερ εἶπον, ἐπὶ τούτοις ἀφίοιτε, D
εἴποιμ' ἂν ὑμῖν ὅτι ἐγὼ ὑμᾶς, ἄνδρες Ἀθηναῖοι, ἀσπάζομαι μὲν καὶ φιλῶ, πείσομαι δὲ μᾶλλον τῷ θεῷ ἢ ὑμῖν,
καὶ ἕωσπερ ἂν ἐμπνέω καὶ οἷός τε ὦ, οὐ μὴ παύσωμαι

The daily conversation of Socrates.

φιλοσοφῶν καὶ ὑμῖν παρακελευόμενός τε καὶ ἐνδεικνύ-
μενος ὅτῳ ἂν ἀεὶ ἐντυγχάνω ὑμῶν, λέγων οἷάπερ εἴωθα,
ὅτι ὦ ἄριστε ἀνδρῶν, Ἀθηναῖος ὤν, πόλεως τῆς μεγίστης
καὶ εὐδοκιμωτάτης εἰς σοφίαν καὶ ἰσχύν, χρημάτων μὲν
οὐκ αἰσχύνει ἐπιμελούμενος, ὅπως σοι ἔσται ὡς πλεῖστα,
καὶ δόξης καὶ τιμῆς, φρονήσεως δὲ καὶ ἀληθείας καὶ τῆς E
ψυχῆς, ὅπως ὡς βελτίστη ἔσται, οὐκ ἐπιμελεῖ οὐδὲ φροντίζεις; καὶ ἐάν τις ὑμῶν ἀμφισβητῇ καὶ φῇ ἐπιμελεῖσθαι,
οὐκ εὐθὺς ἀφήσω αὐτὸν οὐδ' ἄπειμι, ἀλλ' ἐρήσομαι αὐτὸν
καὶ ἐξετάσω καὶ ἐλέγξω, καὶ ἐάν μοι μὴ δοκῇ κεκτῆσθαι
ἀρετήν, φάναι δέ, ὀνειδιῶ ὅτι τὰ πλείστου ἄξια περὶ
ἐλαχίστου ποιεῖται, τὰ δὲ φαυλότερα περὶ πλείονος. ταῦτα 30
καὶ νεωτέρῳ καὶ πρεσβυτέρῳ, ὅτῳ ἂν ἐντυγχάνω, ποιήσω,
καὶ ξένῳ καὶ ἀστῷ, μᾶλλον δὲ τοῖς ἀστοῖς, ὅσῳ μου
ἐγγυτέρω ἐστὲ γένει. ταῦτα γὰρ κελεύει ὁ θεός, εὖ ἴστε,
καὶ ἐγὼ οἴομαι οὐδέν πω ὑμῖν μεῖζον ἀγαθὸν γενέσθαι ἐν
τῇ πόλει ἢ τὴν ἐμὴν τῷ θεῷ ὑπηρεσίαν. οὐδὲν γὰρ ἄλλο
πράττων ἐγὼ περιέρχομαι ἢ πείθων ὑμῶν καὶ νεωτέρους
καὶ πρεσβυτέρους μήτε σωμάτων ἐπιμελεῖσθαι μήτε
χρημάτων πρότερον μηδὲ οὕτω σφόδρα ὡς τῆς ψυχῆς, ὅπως B
ὡς ἀρίστη ἔσται, λέγων ὅτι οὐκ ἐκ χρημάτων ἀρετὴ γίγνεται,
ἀλλ' ἐξ ἀρετῆς χρήματα καὶ τἆλλα ἀγαθὰ τοῖς ἀνθρώποις
ἅπαντα καὶ ἰδίᾳ καὶ δημοσίᾳ. εἰ μὲν οὖν ταῦτα λέγων
διαφθείρω τοὺς νέους, ταῦτ' ἂν εἴη βλαβερά· εἰ δέ τίς μέ
φησιν ἄλλα λέγειν ἢ ταῦτα, οὐδὲν λέγει. πρὸς ταῦτα,

φαίην ἄν, ὦ Ἀθηναῖοι, ἢ πείθεσθε Ἀνύτῳ ἢ μή, καὶ ἢ
ἀφίετε ἢ μὴ ἀφίετε, ὡς ἐμοῦ οὐκ ἂν ποιήσοντος ἄλλα, οὐδ'
C εἰ μέλλω πολλάκις τεθνάναι.

*Hear me patiently, Athenians; for it will do you good. If you
put me to death, you will be injuring yourselves more than me,
and flying in the face of Heaven. You will not easily find
another to awake you from the slumber of self-complacency.
Have I not sacrificed all in your service?*

Μὴ θορυβεῖτε, ἄνδρες Ἀθηναῖοι, ἀλλ' ἐμμείνατέ μοι
οἷς ἐδεήθην ὑμῶν, μὴ θορυβεῖν ἐφ' οἷς ἂν λέγω, ἀλλ'
ἀκούειν· καὶ γάρ, ὡς ἐγὼ οἶμαι, ὀνήσεσθε ἀκούοντες.
μέλλω γὰρ οὖν ἄττα ὑμῖν ἐρεῖν καὶ ἄλλα, ἐφ' οἷς
ἴσως βοήσεσθε· ἀλλὰ μηδαμῶς ποιεῖτε τοῦτο. εὖ γὰρ
ἴστε, ἐὰν ἐμὲ ἀποκτείνητε τοιοῦτον ὄντα, οἷον ἐγὼ
λέγω, οὐκ ἐμὲ μείζω βλάψετε ἢ ὑμᾶς αὐτούς· ἐμὲ μὲν
γὰρ οὐδὲν ἂν βλάψειεν οὔτε Μέλητος οὔτε Ἄνυτος·
D οὐδὲ γὰρ ἂν δύναιτο· οὐ γὰρ οἴομαι θεμιτὸν εἶναι
ἀμείνονι ἀνδρὶ ὑπὸ χείρονος βλάπτεσθαι. ἀποκτείνειε
μέντ' ἂν ἴσως ἢ ἐξελάσειεν ἢ ἀτιμώσειεν· ἀλλὰ ταῦτα
οὗτος ἴσως οἴεται καὶ ἄλλος τίς που μεγάλα κακά, ἐγὼ
δ' οὐκ οἴομαι, ἀλλὰ πολὺ μᾶλλον ποιεῖν ἃ οὗτος νυνὶ
ποιεῖ, ἄνδρα ἀδίκως ἐπιχειρεῖν ἀποκτιννύναι. νῦν οὖν,
ὦ ἄνδρες Ἀθηναῖοι, πολλοῦ δέω ἐγὼ ὑπὲρ ἐμαυτοῦ
ἀπολογεῖσθαι, ὥς τις ἂν οἴοιτο, ἀλλ' ὑπὲρ ὑμῶν, μή τι
ἐξαμάρτητε περὶ τὴν τοῦ θεοῦ δόσιν ὑμῖν ἐμοῦ καταψη-
E φισάμενοι. ἐὰν γὰρ ἐμὲ ἀποκτείνητε, οὐ ῥᾳδίως ἄλλον
τοιοῦτον εὑρήσετε, ἀτεχνῶς, εἰ καὶ γελοιότερον εἰπεῖν, *Simile of
προσκείμενον τῇ πόλει ὑπὸ τοῦ θεοῦ, ὥσπερ ἵππῳ με- and gad-fly.*
γάλῳ μὲν καὶ γενναίῳ, ὑπὸ μεγέθους δὲ νωθεστέρῳ
καὶ δεομένῳ ἐγείρεσθαι ὑπὸ μύωπός τινος· οἷον δή μοι
δοκεῖ ὁ θεὸς ἐμὲ τῇ πόλει προστεθεικέναι τοιοῦτόν τινα,

ὃς ὑμᾶς ἐγείρων καὶ πείθων καὶ ὀνειδίζων ἕνα ἕκαστον οὐδὲν παύομαι τὴν ἡμέραν ὅλην πανταχοῦ προσκαθί- 31 ζων. τοιοῦτος οὖν ἄλλος οὐ ῥᾳδίως ὑμῖν γενήσεται, ὦ ἄνδρες, ἀλλ᾽ ἐὰν ἐμοὶ πείθησθε, φείσεσθέ μου· ὑμεῖς δ᾽ ἴσως τάχ᾽ ἂν ἀχθόμενοι, ὥσπερ οἱ νυστάζοντες ἐγειρόμενοι, κρούσαντες ἄν με, πειθόμενοι Ἀνύτῳ, ῥᾳδίως ἂν ἀποκτείναιτε, εἶτα τὸν λοιπὸν βίον καθεύδοντες διατελοῖτ᾽ ἄν, εἰ μή τινα ἄλλον ὁ θεὸς ὑμῖν ἐπιπέμψειε κηδόμενος ὑμῶν. ὅτι δ᾽ ἐγὼ τυγχάνω ὢν τοιοῦτος, οἷος ὑπὸ τοῦ θεοῦ τῇ πόλει δεδόσθαι, ἐνθένδε ἂν κατανοήσαιτε· οὐ γὰρ ἀνθρωπίνῳ ἔοικε τὸ ἐμὲ τῶν μὲν ἐμαυ- B τοῦ ἁπάντων ἠμεληκέναι καὶ ἀνέχεσθαι τῶν οἰκείων ἀμελουμένων τοσαῦτα ἤδη ἔτη, τὸ δὲ ὑμέτερον πράττειν ἀεί, ἰδίᾳ ἑκάστῳ προσιόντα, ὥσπερ πατέρα ἢ ἀδελφὸν πρεσβύτερον, πείθοντα ἐπιμελεῖσθαι ἀρετῆς. καὶ εἰ μέν [τι] ἀπὸ τούτων ἀπέλαυον καὶ μισθὸν λαμβάνων ταῦτα παρεκελευόμην, εἶχον ἄν τινα λόγον· νῦν δὲ ὁρᾶτε δὴ καὶ αὐτοί, ὅτι οἱ κατήγοροι τἆλλα πάντα ἀναισχύντως οὕτω κατηγοροῦντες τοῦτό γε οὐχ οἷοί τε ἐγένοντο ἀπαναισχυντῆσαι, παρασχόμενοι μάρτυρα, ὡς ἐγώ ποτέ C τινα ἢ ἐπραξάμην μισθὸν ἢ ᾔτησα. ἱκανὸν γάρ, οἶμαι, ἐγὼ παρέχομαι τὸν μάρτυρα, ἀληθῆ ὡς λέγω, τὴν πενίαν.

That I have not addressed you in public is due to the divine sign, which has deterred me from a course which could only end in my destruction.

Reason why Socrates did not take to politics, 31 C-33 A.

Ἴσως ἂν οὖν δόξειεν ἄτοπον εἶναι, ὅτι δὴ ἐγὼ ἰδίᾳ μὲν ταῦτα ξυμβουλεύω περιιὼν καὶ πολυπραγμονῶ, δημοσίᾳ δὲ οὐ τολμῶ ἀναβαίνων εἰς τὸ πλῆθος τὸ ὑμέτερον ξυμβουλεύειν τῇ πόλει. τούτου δὲ αἴτιόν ἐστιν ὃ ὑμεῖς ἐμοῦ πολλάκις ἀκηκόατε πολλαχοῦ λέγοντος,

D ὅτι μοι θεῖόν τι καὶ δαιμόνιον γίγνεται [φωνή], ὃ δὴ The
καὶ ἐν τῇ γραφῇ ἐπικωμῳδῶν Μέλητος ἐγράψατο· ἐμοὶ δαιμόνιον.
δὲ τοῦτ᾽ ἐστὶν ἐκ παιδὸς ἀρξάμενον, φωνή τις γιγνομένη,
ἣ ὅταν γένηται, ἀεὶ ἀποτρέπει με τούτου, ὃ ἂν
μέλλω πράττειν, προτρέπει δὲ οὔποτε· τοῦτ᾽ ἔστιν ὅ
μοι ἐναντιοῦται τὰ πολιτικὰ πράττειν. καὶ παγκάλως
γέ μοι δοκεῖ ἐναντιοῦσθαι· εὖ γὰρ ἴστε, ὦ ἄνδρες
Ἀθηναῖοι, εἰ ἐγὼ [πάλαι] ἐπεχείρησα πράττειν τὰ πολιτικὰ πράγματα, πάλαι ἂν ἀπολώλη καὶ οὔτ᾽ ἂν
E ὑμᾶς ὠφελήκη οὐδὲν οὔτ᾽ ἂν ἐμαυτόν. καί μοι μὴ
ἄχθεσθε λέγοντι τἀληθῆ· οὐ γὰρ ἔστιν ὅστις ἀνθρώπων σωθήσεται οὔτε ὑμῖν οὔτε ἄλλῳ πλήθει οὐδενὶ
γνησίως ἐναντιούμενος καὶ διακωλύων πολλὰ ἄδικα
32 καὶ παράνομα ἐν τῇ πόλει γίγνεσθαι, ἀλλ᾽ ἀναγκαῖόν
ἐστι τὸν τῷ ὄντι μαχούμενον ὑπὲρ τοῦ δικαίου, καὶ εἰ
μέλλει ὀλίγον χρόνον σωθήσεσθαι, ἰδιωτεύειν ἀλλὰ μὴ
δημοσιεύειν.

*When I have acted in a public capacity, it has been at the risk of
my life. I maintained the right in the teeth of the Democracy,
and again of the Thirty Tyrants.*

Μεγάλα δ᾽ ἔγωγε ὑμῖν τεκμήρια παρέξομαι τούτων, οὐ λόγους, ἀλλ᾽ ὃ ὑμεῖς τιμᾶτε, ἔργα. ἀκούσατε
δή μου τὰ ἐμοὶ ξυμβεβηκότα, ἵν᾽ εἰδῆτε ὅτι οὐδ᾽ ἂν
ἑνὶ ὑπεικάθοιμι παρὰ τὸ δίκαιον δείσας θάνατον, μὴ
ὑπείκων δὲ ἅμα καὶ ἅμ᾽ ἂν ἀπολοίμην. ἐρῶ δὲ ὑμῖν Conduct o
φορτικὰ μὲν καὶ δικανικά, ἀληθῆ δέ. ἐγὼ γάρ, ὦ Socrates a
the trial o
B Ἀθηναῖοι, ἄλλην μὲν ἀρχὴν οὐδεμίαν πώποτε ἦρξα ἐν the general
τῇ πόλει, ἐβούλευσα δέ· καὶ ἔτυχεν ἡμῶν ἡ φυλὴ [Ἀν- after the
τιοχὶς] πρυτανεύουσα, ὅτε ὑμεῖς τοὺς δέκα στρατηγοὺς Arginusae
τοὺς οὐκ ἀνελομένους τοὺς ἐκ τῆς ναυμαχίας ἐβούλεσθε
ἀθρόους κρίνειν, παρανόμως, ὡς ἐν τῷ ὑστέρῳ χρόνῳ

πᾶσιν ὑμῖν ἔδοξε. τότ' ἐγὼ μόνος τῶν πρυτάνεων ἠναντιώθην [ὑμῖν] μηδὲν ποιεῖν παρὰ τοὺς νόμους [καὶ ἐναντία ἐψηφισάμην], καὶ ἑτοίμων ὄντων ἐνδεικνύναι με καὶ ἀπάγειν τῶν ῥητόρων, καὶ ὑμῶν κελευόντων καὶ βοώντων, μετὰ τοῦ νόμου καὶ τοῦ δικαίου ᾤμην μᾶλλόν με C δεῖν διακινδυνεύειν ἢ μεθ' ὑμῶν γενέσθαι μὴ δίκαια βουλευομένων, φοβηθέντα δεσμὸν ἢ θάνατον. καὶ ταῦτα μὲν ἦν ἔτι δημοκρατουμένης τῆς πόλεως· ἐπειδὴ δὲ ὀλιγαρχία ἐγένετο, οἱ τριάκοντα αὖ μεταπεμψάμενοί με πέμπτον αὐτὸν εἰς τὴν θόλον προσέταξαν ἀγαγεῖν ἐκ Σαλαμῖνος Λέοντα τὸν Σαλαμίνιον, ἵν' ἀποθάνοι· οἷα δὴ καὶ ἄλλοις ἐκεῖνοι πολλοῖς πολλὰ προσέταττον, βουλόμενοι ὡς πλείστους ἀναπλῆσαι αἰτιῶν· τότε μέντοι ἐγὼ οὐ λόγῳ ἀλλ' ἔργῳ αὖ ἐνεδειξάμην, ὅτι ἐμοὶ θανάτου D μὲν μέλει, εἰ μὴ ἀγροικότερον ἦν εἰπεῖν, οὐδ' ὁτιοῦν, τοῦ δὲ μηδὲν ἄδικον μηδ' ἀνόσιον ἐργάζεσθαι, τούτου δὲ τὸ πᾶν μέλει. ἐμὲ γὰρ ἐκείνη ἡ ἀρχὴ οὐκ ἐξέπληξεν οὕτως ἰσχυρὰ οὖσα, ὥστε ἄδικόν τι ἐργάσασθαι, ἀλλ' ἐπειδὴ ἐκ τῆς θόλου ἐξήλθομεν, οἱ μὲν τέτταρες ᾤχοντο εἰς Σαλαμῖνα καὶ ἤγαγον Λέοντα, ἐγὼ δὲ ᾠχόμην ἀπιὼν οἴκαδε. καὶ ἴσως ἂν διὰ ταῦτ' ἀπέθανον, εἰ μὴ ἡ ἀρχὴ διὰ ταχέων κατελύθη· καὶ τούτων ὑμῖν ἔσονται E πολλοὶ μάρτυρες.

Could I have survived to this age, if I had attempted a public career, acting, as I should have done on these principles? For neither in public nor in private have I ever swerved from the right, nor connived at such conduct in others. I have never received pay for speaking, nor selected my audience, and I cannot be held responsible for the conduct of those who may have chanced to listen to me.

Ἆρ' οὖν ἄν με οἴεσθε τοσάδε ἔτη διαγενέσθαι, εἰ

Refusal of Socrates to assist in the arrest of Leon.

ἔπραττον τὰ δημόσια, καὶ πράττων ἀξίως ἀνδρὸς ἀγαθοῦ ἐβοήθουν τοῖς δικαίοις καί, ὥσπερ χρή, τοῦτο περὶ πλείστου ἐποιούμην; πολλοῦ γε δεῖ, ὦ ἄνδρες Ἀθηναῖοι. οὐδὲ γὰρ ἂν ἄλλος ἀνθρώπων οὐδείς. ἀλλ' ἐγὼ 33 διὰ παντὸς τοῦ βίου δημοσίᾳ τε, εἴ πού τι ἔπραξα, τοιοῦτος φανοῦμαι, καὶ ἰδίᾳ ὁ αὐτὸς οὗτος, οὐδενὶ πώποτε ξυγχωρήσας οὐδὲν παρὰ τὸ δίκαιον οὔτε ἄλλῳ οὔτε τούτων οὐδενί, οὓς οἱ διαβάλλοντές μέ φασιν ἐμοὺς μαθητὰς εἶναι. ἐγὼ δὲ διδάσκαλος μὲν οὐδενὸς πώποτ' ἐγενόμην· εἰ δέ τίς μου λέγοντος καὶ τὰ ἐμαυτοῦ πράττοντος ἐπιθυμεῖ ἀκούειν, εἴτε νεώτερος εἴτε πρεσβύτερος, οὐδενὶ πώποτε ἐφθόνησα, οὐδὲ χρήματα B μὲν λαμβάνων διαλέγομαι, μὴ λαμβάνων δ' οὔ, ἀλλ' ὁμοίως καὶ πλουσίῳ καὶ πένητι παρέχω ἐμαυτὸν ἐρωτᾶν, καὶ ἐάν τις βούληται ἀποκρινόμενος ἀκούειν ὧν ἂν λέγω. καὶ τούτων ἐγὼ εἴτε τις χρηστὸς γίγνεται εἴτε μή, οὐκ ἂν δικαίως τὴν αἰτίαν ὑπέχοιμι, ὧν μήτε ὑπεσχόμην μηδενὶ μηδὲν πώποτε μάθημα μήτε ἐδίδαξα· εἰ δέ τίς φησι παρ' ἐμοῦ πώποτέ τι μαθεῖν ἢ ἀκοῦσαι ἰδίᾳ ὅ τι μὴ καὶ οἱ ἄλλοι πάντες, εὖ ἴστε ὅτι οὐκ ἀληθῆ λέγει.

The young men, I confess, take pleasure in hearing me examine pretenders to wisdom: but this with me is a divine mission. If I am the corrupter of youth, why are not witnesses brought to prove it from among my circle of associates? Why are the friends of those I have corrupted—men of mature age and established character—here to defend me?

Ἀλλὰ διὰ τί δή ποτε μετ' ἐμοῦ χαίρουσί τινες πολὺν C χρόνον διατρίβοντες; ἀκηκόατε, ὦ ἄνδρες Ἀθηναῖοι· πᾶσαν ὑμῖν τὴν ἀλήθειαν ἐγὼ εἶπον, ὅτι ἀκούοντες χαίρουσιν ἐξεταζομένοις τοῖς οἰομένοις μὲν εἶναι σοφοῖς, οὖσι δ' οὔ· ἔστι γὰρ οὐκ ἀηδές. ἐμοὶ δὲ τοῦτο,

Divine mission of Socrates.

ὡς ἐγώ φημι, προστέτακται ὑπὸ τοῦ θεοῦ πράττειν καὶ ἐκ μαντείων καὶ ἐξ ἐνυπνίων καὶ παντὶ τρόπῳ, ᾧπερ τίς ποτε καὶ ἄλλη θεία μοῖρα ἀνθρώπῳ καὶ ὁτιοῦν προσέταξε πράττειν. ταῦτα, ὦ Ἀθηναῖοι, καὶ ἀληθῆ ἐστὶ καὶ εὐέλεγκτα. εἰ γὰρ δὴ ἔγωγε τῶν νέων τοὺς μὲν διαφθείρω, τοὺς δὲ διέφθαρκα, χρῆν δήπου, εἴτε τινὲς D αὐτῶν πρεσβύτεροι γενόμενοι ἔγνωσαν ὅτι νέοις οὖσιν αὐτοῖς ἐγὼ κακὸν πώποτέ τι ξυνεβούλευσα, νυνὶ αὐτοὺς ἀναβαίνοντας ἐμοῦ κατηγορεῖν καὶ τιμωρεῖσθαι· εἰ δὲ μὴ αὐτοὶ ἤθελον, τῶν οἰκείων τινὰς τῶν ἐκείνων, πατέρας καὶ ἀδελφοὺς καὶ ἄλλους τοὺς προσήκοντας, εἴπερ ὑπ᾽ ἐμοῦ τι κακὸν ἐπεπόνθεσαν αὐτῶν οἱ οἰκεῖοι, νῦν μεμνῆσθαι καὶ τιμωρεῖσθαι.

The companions of Socrates.

πάντως δὲ πάρεισιν αὐτῶν πολλοὶ ἐνταυθοῖ, οὓς ἐγὼ ὁρῶ, πρῶτον μὲν Κρίτων οὑτοσί, ἐμὸς ἡλικιώτης καὶ δημότης, Κριτοβούλου τοῦδε E πατήρ· ἔπειτα Λυσανίας ὁ Σφήττιος, Αἰσχίνου τοῦδε πατήρ· ἔτι Ἀντιφῶν ὁ Κηφισιεὺς οὑτοσί, Ἐπιγένους πατήρ· ἄλλοι τοίνυν οὗτοι, ὧν οἱ ἀδελφοὶ ἐν ταύτῃ τῇ διατριβῇ γεγόνασι, Νικόστρατος, ὁ Θεοζοτίδου, ἀδελφὸς Θεοδότου— καὶ ὁ μὲν Θεόδοτος τετελεύτηκεν, ὥστε οὐκ ἂν ἐκεῖνός γε αὐτοῦ καταδεηθείη —, καὶ Πάραλος ὅδε, ὁ Δημοδόκου, οὗ ἦν Θεάγης ἀδελφός· ὅδε δὲ Ἀδεί- 34 μαντος, ὁ Ἀρίστωνος, οὗ ἀδελφὸς οὑτοσὶ Πλάτων, καὶ Αἰαντόδωρος, οὗ Ἀπολλόδωρος ὅδε ἀδελφός. καὶ ἄλλους πολλοὺς ἐγὼ ἔχω ὑμῖν εἰπεῖν, ὧν τινὰ ἐχρῆν μάλιστα μὲν ἐν τῷ ἑαυτοῦ λόγῳ παρασχέσθαι Μέλητον μάρτυρα· εἰ δὲ τότε ἐπελάθετο, νῦν παρασχέσθω, ἐγὼ παραχωρῶ, καὶ λεγέτω, εἴ τι ἔχει τοιοῦτον. ἀλλὰ τούτου πᾶν τοὐναντίον εὑρήσετε, ὦ ἄνδρες, πάντας ἐμοὶ βοηθεῖν ἑτοίμους τῷ διαφθείροντι, τῷ κακὰ ἐργαζομένῳ τοὺς οἰκείους αὐτῶν, ὥς φασι Μέλητος καὶ Ἄνυτος. αὐτοὶ μὲν B γὰρ οἱ διεφθαρμένοι τάχ' ἂν λόγον ἔχοιεν βοηθοῦντες· οἱ δὲ ἀδιάφθαρτοι, πρεσβύτεροι ἤδη ἄνδρες, οἱ τούτων προσήκοντες, τίνα ἄλλον ἔχουσι λόγον βοηθοῦντες ἐμοὶ ἀλλ' ἢ τὸν ὀρθόν τε καὶ δίκαιον, ὅτι ξυνίσασι Μελήτῳ μὲν ψευδομένῳ, ἐμοὶ δὲ ἀληθεύοντι;

5. The Peroration, 34 B–35 D.

Some of you might perhaps be inclined to judge me harshly, because I have not brought forward my children, and appealed to the court for mercy. Such appeals seem to me to be unworthy of a man, and still more unworthy of the State.

Εἶεν δή, ὦ ἄνδρες· ἃ μὲν ἐγὼ ἔχοιμ' ἂν ἀπολο- C γεῖσθαι, σχεδόν ἐστι ταῦτα καὶ ἄλλα ἴσως τοιαῦτα. τάχα δ' ἄν τις ὑμῶν ἀγανακτήσειεν ἀναμνησθεὶς ἑαυτοῦ, εἰ ὁ μὲν καὶ ἐλάττω τουτουὶ τοῦ ἀγῶνος ἀγῶνα ἀγωνιζό- μενος ἐδεήθη τε καὶ ἱκέτευσε τοὺς δικαστὰς μετὰ πολλῶν δακρύων, παιδία τε αὑτοῦ ἀναβιβασάμενος, ἵνα ὅ τι μάλιστα ἐλεηθείη, καὶ ἄλλους τῶν οἰκείων καὶ φίλων πολλούς, ἐγὼ δὲ οὐδὲν ἄρα τούτων ποιήσω, καὶ ταῦτα κινδυνεύων, ὡς ἂν δόξαιμι, τὸν ἔσχατον κίνδυνον. τάχ' οὖν τις ταῦτα ἐννοήσας αὐθαδέστερον ἂν πρός με σχοίη, καὶ ὀργισθεὶς αὐτοῖς τούτοις θεῖτο ἂν μετ' ὀργῆς τὴν D ψῆφον. εἰ δή τις ὑμῶν οὕτως ἔχει, — οὐκ ἀξιῶ μὲν γὰρ ἔγωγε· εἰ δ' οὖν, ἐπιεικῆ ἄν μοι δοκῶ πρὸς τοῦτον λέγειν λέγων ὅτι ἐμοί, ὦ ἄριστε, εἰσὶ μέν πού τινες καὶ οἰκεῖοι· καὶ γὰρ τοῦτο αὐτὸ τὸ τοῦ Ὁμήρου, οὐδ' ἐγὼ ἀπὸ δρυὸς οὐδ' ἀπὸ πέτρης πέφυκα, ἀλλ' ἐξ ἀνθρώπων, ὥστε καὶ οἰκεῖοί μοί εἰσι καὶ υἱεῖς, ὦ ἄνδρες Ἀθηναῖοι, τρεῖς, εἷς μὲν μειράκιον ἤδη, δύο δὲ παιδία· ἀλλ' ὅμως οὐδέν' αὐτῶν δεῦρο ἀναβιβασά- μενος δεήσομαι ὑμῶν ἀποψηφίσασθαι. τί δὴ οὖν οὐδὲν E τούτων ποιήσω; οὐκ αὐθαδιζόμενος, ὦ ἄνδρες Ἀθηναῖοι, οὐδ' ὑμᾶς ἀτιμάζων, ἀλλ' εἰ μὲν θαρραλέως ἐγὼ ἔχω πρὸς

Reasons for not entreating the mercy of the court (1) Such a course is not dignified.

θανάτου ἢ μή, ἄλλος λόγος, πρὸς δ᾽ οὖν δόξαν καὶ ἐμοὶ καὶ ὑμῖν καὶ ὅλῃ τῇ πόλει οὔ μοι δοκεῖ καλὸν εἶναι ἐμὲ τούτων οὐδὲν ποιεῖν καὶ τηλικόνδε ὄντα καὶ τοῦτο τοὔνομα ἔχοντα, εἴτ᾽ οὖν ἀληθὲς εἴτ᾽ οὖν ψεῦδος· ἀλλ᾽ οὖν δεδογμένον γέ ἐστι τὸ Σωκράτη διαφέρειν τινὶ τῶν πολλῶν ἀνθρώπων. εἰ οὖν ὑμῶν οἱ δοκοῦντες διαφέρειν εἴτε σοφίᾳ εἴτε ἀνδρείᾳ 35 εἴτε ἄλλῃ ᾑτινιοῦν ἀρετῇ τοιοῦτοι ἔσονται, αἰσχρὸν ἂν εἴη· οἷονπερ ἐγὼ πολλάκις ἑώρακά τινας, ὅταν κρίνωνται, δοκοῦντας μέν τι εἶναι, θαυμάσια δὲ ἐργαζομένους, ὡς δεινόν τι οἰομένους πείσεσθαι εἰ ἀποθανοῦνται, ὥσπερ ἀθανάτων ἐσομένων, ἂν ὑμεῖς αὐτοὺς μὴ ἀποκτείνητε· οἳ ἐμοὶ δοκοῦσιν αἰσχύνην τῇ πόλει περιάπτειν, ὥστ᾽ ἄν τινα καὶ τῶν ξένων ὑπολαβεῖν ὅτι οἱ διαφέροντες Ἀθηναίων B εἰς ἀρετήν, οὓς αὐτοὶ ἑαυτῶν ἔν τε ταῖς ἀρχαῖς καὶ ταῖς ἄλλαις τιμαῖς προκρίνουσιν, οὗτοι γυναικῶν οὐδὲν διαφέρουσι. ταῦτα γάρ, ὦ ἄνδρες Ἀθηναῖοι, οὔτε ἡμᾶς χρὴ ποιεῖν τοὺς δοκοῦντας καὶ ὁτιοῦν εἶναι, οὔτ᾽, ἂν ἡμεῖς ποιῶμεν, ὑμᾶς ἐπιτρέπειν, ἀλλὰ τοῦτο αὐτὸ ἐνδείκνυσθαι, ὅτι πολὺ μᾶλλον καταψηφιεῖσθε τοῦ τὰ ἐλεεινὰ ταῦτα δράματα εἰσάγοντος καὶ καταγέλαστον τὴν πόλιν ποιοῦντος ἢ τοῦ ἡσυχίαν ἄγοντος.

Besides it is not right for you to listen to appeals. It is your business to be just. If I tried to make you vote against your consciences, I should deserve the name of atheist.

(2) It is not right

Χωρὶς δὲ τῆς δόξης, ὦ ἄνδρες, οὐδὲ δίκαιόν μοι δοκεῖ εἶναι δεῖσθαι τοῦ δικαστοῦ οὐδὲ δεόμενον ἀποφεύγειν, C ἀλλὰ διδάσκειν καὶ πείθειν. οὐ γὰρ ἐπὶ τούτῳ κάθηται ὁ δικαστής, ἐπὶ τῷ καταχαρίζεσθαι τὰ δίκαια, ἀλλ᾽ ἐπὶ τῷ κρίνειν ταῦτα· καὶ ὀμώμοκεν οὐ χαριεῖσθαι οἷς ἂν δοκῇ αὐτῷ, ἀλλὰ δικάσειν κατὰ τοὺς νόμους. οὔκουν χρὴ οὔτε ἡμᾶς ἐθίζειν ὑμᾶς ἐπιορκεῖν, οὔθ᾽ ὑμᾶς ἐθίζεσθαι· οὐδέτεροι γὰρ ἂν ἡμῶν εὐσεβοῖεν. μὴ οὖν ἀξιοῦτέ με, ὦ ἄνδρες Ἀθηναῖοι, τοιαῦτα δεῖν πρὸς ὑμᾶς πράττειν, ἃ μήτε ἡγοῦμαι καλὰ εἶναι μήτε δίκαια μήτε D ὅσια, ἄλλως τε μέντοι νὴ Δία πάντως καὶ ἀσεβείας φεύγοντα ὑπὸ Μελήτου τουτουί. σαφῶς γὰρ ἄν, εἰ πείθοιμι ὑμᾶς καὶ τῷ δεῖσθαι βιαζοίμην ὀμωμοκότας, θεοὺς ἂν διδάσκοιμι μὴ ἡγεῖσθαι ὑμᾶς εἶναι, καὶ ἀτεχνῶς ἀπολογούμενος κατηγοροίην ἂν ἐμαυτοῦ ὡς θεοὺς οὐ νομίζω. ἀλλὰ πολλοῦ δεῖ οὕτως ἔχειν· νομίζω τε γάρ, ὦ ἄνδρες Ἀθηναῖοι, ὡς οὐδεὶς τῶν ἐμῶν κατηγόρων, καὶ ὑμῖν ἐπιτρέπω καὶ τῷ θεῷ κρῖναι περὶ ἐμοῦ ὅπῃ μέλλει ἐμοί τε ἄριστα εἶναι καὶ ὑμῖν.

(The votes are given, and Socrates is condemned.)

II. THE COUNTER-ASSESSMENT.

The majority against me is small. It is well for Meletus that he had the support of Anytus and Lycon, else he would have had to pay the fine.

E Τὸ μὲν μὴ ἀγανακτεῖν, ὦ ἄνδρες Ἀθηναῖοι, ἐπὶ τούτῳ 36 τῷ γεγονότι, ὅτι μου κατεψηφίσασθε, ἄλλα τέ μοι πολλὰ ξυμβάλλεται, καὶ οὐκ ἀνέλπιστόν μοι γέγονε τὸ γεγονὸς τοῦτο, ἀλλὰ πολὺ μᾶλλον θαυμάζω ἑκατέρων τῶν ψήφων τὸν γεγονότα ἀριθμόν. οὐ γὰρ ᾤμην ἔγωγε οὕτω παρ' ὀλίγον ἔσεσθαι, ἀλλὰ παρὰ πολύ· νῦν δέ, ὡς ἔοικεν, εἰ τριάκοντα μόναι μετέπεσον τῶν ψήφων, ἀποπεφεύγη ἄν. Μέλητον μὲν οὖν, ὡς ἐμοὶ δοκῶ, καὶ νῦν ἀποπέφευγα, καὶ οὐ μόνον ἀποπέφευγα, ἀλλὰ παντὶ δῆλον τοῦτό γε, ὅτι, εἰ μὴ ἀνέβησαν Ἄνυτος καὶ Λύκων κατη-B γορήσοντες ἐμοῦ, κἂν ὦφλε χιλίας δραχμάς, οὐ μεταλαβὼν τὸ πέμπτον μέρος τῶν ψήφων.

Smallness of the majority against Socrates.

The penalty is fixed at death. What alternative do I propose? If justice were really to be done to me, I should be supported at the public expense.

His proposal that he should be maintained free of expense in the Prytaneum.

Τιμᾶται δ' οὖν μοι ὁ ἀνὴρ θανάτου. εἶεν· ἐγὼ δὲ δὴ τίνος ὑμῖν ἀντιτιμήσωμαι, ὦ ἄνδρες Ἀθηναῖοι; ἢ δῆλον ὅτι τῆς ἀξίας; τί οὖν; τί ἄξιός εἰμι παθεῖν ἢ ἀποτῖσαι, ὅ τι μαθὼν ἐν τῷ βίῳ οὐχ ἡσυχίαν ἦγον, ἀλλ' ἀμελήσας ὧνπερ οἱ πολλοί, χρηματισμοῦ τε καὶ οἰκονομίας καὶ στρατηγιῶν καὶ δημηγοριῶν καὶ τῶν ἄλλων ἀρχῶν καὶ ξυνωμοσιῶν καὶ στάσεων τῶν ἐν τῇ πόλει γιγνομένων, ἡγησάμενος ἐμαυτὸν τῷ ὄντι ἐπιεικέστερον εἶναι ἢ ὥστε εἰς ταῦτ' ἰόντα σώζεσθαι, ἐνταῦθα μὲν οὐκ ᾖα, C οἷ ἐλθὼν μήτε ὑμῖν μήτε ἐμαυτῷ ἔμελλον μηδὲν ὄφελος εἶναι, ἐπὶ δὲ τὸ ἰδίᾳ ἕκαστον ἰὼν εὐεργετεῖν τὴν μεγίστην εὐεργεσίαν, ὡς ἐγώ φημι, [ἐνταῦθα ᾖα,] ἐπιχειρῶν ἕκαστον ὑμῶν πείθειν μὴ πρότερον μήτε τῶν ἑαυτοῦ μηδενὸς ἐπιμελεῖσθαι, πρὶν ἑαυτοῦ ἐπιμεληθείη, ὅπως ὡς βέλτιστος καὶ φρονιμώτατος ἔσοιτο, μήτε τῶν τῆς πόλεως, πρὶν αὐτῆς τῆς πόλεως, τῶν τε ἄλλων οὕτω κατὰ τὸν αὐτὸν τρόπον ἐπιμελεῖσθαι· τί οὖν εἰμὶ ἄξιος παθεῖν τοιοῦτος ὤν; ἀγαθόν τι, ὦ ἄνδρες Ἀθηναῖοι, εἰ δεῖ γε κατὰ τὴν ἀξίαν D τῇ ἀληθείᾳ τιμᾶσθαι· καὶ ταῦτά γε ἀγαθὸν τοιοῦτον, ὅ τι ἂν πρέποι ἐμοί. τί οὖν πρέπει ἀνδρὶ πένητι εὐεργέτῃ, δεομένῳ ἄγειν σχολὴν ἐπὶ τῇ ὑμετέρᾳ παρακελεύσει; οὐκ ἔσθ' ὅ τι μᾶλλον, ὦ ἄνδρες Ἀθηναῖοι, πρέπει οὕτως, ὡς τὸν τοιοῦτον ἄνδρα ἐν πρυτανείῳ σιτεῖσθαι, πολύ γε μᾶλλον ἢ εἴ τις ὑμῶν ἵππῳ ἢ ξυνωρίδι ἢ ζεύγει νενίκηκεν Ὀλυμπίασιν. ὁ μὲν γὰρ ὑμᾶς ποιεῖ εὐδαίμονας δοκεῖν [εἶναι], ἐγὼ δὲ εἶναι· καὶ ὁ μὲν τροφῆς οὐδὲν δεῖται, ἐγὼ E δὲ δέομαι. εἰ οὖν δεῖ με κατὰ τὸ δίκαιον τῆς ἀξίας 37 τιμᾶσθαι, τούτου τιμῶμαι, ἐν πρυτανείῳ σιτήσεως.

APOLOGY, 37 A–D.

Do not think me insolent. But I cannot admit that I am deserving of evil. Now imprisonment and exile are certainly evils, whereas death may be a good. I will not therefore prefer either of the former. To go into exile would be merely to invite elsewhere the same treatment that I have met with here.

Ἴσως οὖν ὑμῖν καὶ ταυτὶ λέγων παραπλησίως δοκῶ λέγειν ὥσπερ περὶ τοῦ οἴκτου καὶ τῆς ἀντιβολήσεως, ἀπαυθαδιζόμενος· τὸ δὲ οὐκ ἔστιν, ὦ Ἀθηναῖοι, τοιοῦτον, ἀλλὰ τοιόνδε μᾶλλον. πέπεισμαι ἐγὼ ἑκὼν εἶναι μηδένα ἀδικεῖν ἀνθρώπων, ἀλλὰ ὑμᾶς τοῦτο οὐ πείθω· ὀλίγον γὰρ χρόνον ἀλλήλοις διειλέγμεθα· ἐπεί, ὡς ἐγᾦμαι, εἰ ἦν ὑμῖν νόμος, ὥσπερ καὶ ἄλλοις ἀνθρώποις, B περὶ θανάτου μὴ μίαν ἡμέραν μόνον κρίνειν, ἀλλὰ πολλάς, ἐπείσθητε ἄν· νῦν δ᾽ οὐ ῥᾴδιον ἐν χρόνῳ ὀλίγῳ μεγάλας διαβολὰς ἀπολύεσθαι. πεπεισμένος δὴ ἐγὼ μηδένα ἀδικεῖν πολλοῦ δέω ἐμαυτόν γε ἀδικήσειν καὶ κατ᾽ ἐμαυτοῦ ἐρεῖν αὐτός, ὡς ἄξιός εἰμί του κακοῦ καὶ τιμήσεσθαι τοιούτου τινὸς ἐμαυτῷ, τί δείσας; ἢ μὴ πάθω τοῦτο, οὗ Μέλητός μοι τιμᾶται, ὅ φημι οὐκ εἰδέναι οὔτ᾽ εἰ ἀγαθὸν οὔτ᾽ εἰ κακόν ἐστιν; ἀντὶ τούτου δὴ ἕλωμαι ὧν εὖ οἶδ᾽ ὅτι κακῶν ὄντων, τούτου τιμησάμενος; πότερον δεσμοῦ; καὶ τί με δεῖ ζῆν ἐν δεσμωC τηρίῳ, δουλεύοντα τῇ ἀεὶ καθισταμένῃ ἀρχῇ[, τοῖς ἕνδεκα]; ἀλλὰ χρημάτων, καὶ δεδέσθαι ἕως ἂν ἐκτίσω; ἀλλὰ ταὐτόν μοί ἐστιν, ὅπερ νῦν δὴ ἔλεγον· οὐ γὰρ ἔστι μοι χρήματα, ὁπόθεν ἐκτίσω. ἀλλὰ δὴ φυγῆς τιμήσωμαι; ἴσως γὰρ ἄν μοι τούτου τιμήσαιτε. πολλὴ μέντ᾽ ἄν με φιλοψυχία ἔχοι, εἰ οὕτως ἀλόγιστός εἰμι, ὥστε μὴ δύνασθαι λογίζεσθαι, ὅτι ὑμεῖς μὲν ὄντες πολῖταί μου οὐχ οἷοί τε ἐγένεσθε ἐνεγκεῖν τὰς ἐμὰς διατριD βὰς καὶ τοὺς λόγους, ἀλλ᾽ ὑμῖν βαρύτεραι γεγόνασι καὶ

He will not admit himself to be deserving either of imprisonment or exile.

ἐπιφθονώτεραι, ὥστε ζητεῖτε αὐτῶν νυνὶ ἀπαλλαγῆναι, ἄλλοι δὲ ἄρα αὐτὰς οἴσουσι ῥᾳδίως. πολλοῦ γε δεῖ, ὦ Ἀθηναῖοι. καλὸς οὖν ἄν μοι ὁ βίος εἴη ἐξελθόντι τηλικῷδε ἀνθρώπῳ ἄλλην ἐξ ἄλλης πόλιν πόλεως ἀμειβομένῳ καὶ ἐξελαυνομένῳ ζῆν. εὖ γὰρ οἶδ᾽ ὅτι, ὅποι ἂν ἔλθω, λέγοντος ἐμοῦ ἀκροάσονται οἱ νέοι ὥσπερ ἐνθάδε· κἂν μὲν τούτους ἀπελαύνω, οὗτοι ἐμὲ αὐτοὶ ἐξελῶσι, πείθοντες τοὺς πρεσβυτέρους· ἐὰν δὲ μὴ ἀπελαύνω, οἱ E τούτων πατέρες τε καὶ οἰκεῖοι δι᾽ αὐτοὺς τούτους.

'*Well, can you not go away and be silent?*' *No: that would be to disobey the divine command, little as you may believe me when I say it. A money fine I have no objection to, for that is no evil. Perhaps I could manage to pay you a mina of silver. My friends here tell me to say thirty minae, and offer themselves as bail.*

Ἴσως οὖν ἄν τις εἴποι· σιγῶν δὲ καὶ ἡσυχίαν ἄγων, ὦ Σώκρατες, οὐχ οἷός τ᾽ ἔσει ἡμῖν ἐξελθὼν ζῆν; τουτὶ δή ἐστι πάντων χαλεπώτατον πεῖσαί τινας ὑμῶν. ἐάν τε γὰρ λέγω ὅτι τῷ θεῷ ἀπειθεῖν τοῦτ᾽ ἐστὶ καὶ διὰ τοῦτ᾽ ἀδύνατον ἡσυχίαν ἄγειν, οὐ πείσεσθέ μοι ὡς εἰρωνευομένῳ· ἐάν τ᾽ αὖ λέγω ὅτι καὶ τυγχάνει μέγιστον 38 ἀγαθὸν ὂν ἀνθρώπῳ τοῦτο, ἑκάστης ἡμέρας περὶ ἀρετῆς τοὺς λόγους ποιεῖσθαι καὶ τῶν ἄλλων, περὶ ὧν ὑμεῖς ἐμοῦ ἀκούετε διαλεγομένου καὶ ἐμαυτὸν καὶ ἄλλους ἐξετάζοντος, ὁ δὲ ἀνεξέταστος βίος οὐ βιωτὸς ἀνθρώπῳ, ταῦτα δ᾽ ἔτι ἧττον πείσεσθέ μοι λέγοντι. τὰ δὲ ἔχει μὲν οὕτως, ὡς ἐγώ φημι, ὦ ἄνδρες, πείθειν δὲ οὐ ῥᾴδιον. καὶ ἐγὼ ἅμ᾽ οὐκ εἴθισμαι ἐμαυτὸν ἀξιοῦν κακοῦ οὐδενός. εἰ μὲν γὰρ ἦν μοι χρήματα, ἐτιμησάμην ἂν χρημάτων ὅσα ἔμελλον ἐκτίσειν· οὐδὲν γὰρ ἂν ἐβλά- B βην· νῦν δέ — οὐ γὰρ ἔστιν, εἰ μὴ ἄρα ὅσον ἂν ἐγὼ

but is willing to pay a fine,

δυναίμην ἐκτῖσαι, τοσούτου βούλεσθέ μοι τιμῆσαι. ἴσως
δ' ἂν δυναίμην ἐκτῖσαι ὑμῖν μνᾶν ἀργυρίου· τοσούτου
οὖν τιμῶμαι. Πλάτων δὲ ὅδε, ὦ ἄνδρες Ἀθηναῖοι, καὶ *in which his friends will help him.*
Κρίτων καὶ Κριτόβουλος καὶ Ἀπολλόδωρος κελεύουσί με
τριάκοντα μνῶν τιμήσασθαι, αὐτοὶ δ' ἐγγυᾶσθαι· τιμῶμαι
C οὖν τοσούτου, ἐγγυηταὶ δ' ὑμῖν ἔσονται τοῦ ἀργυρίου οὗτοι
ἀξιόχρεῳ.

(The penalty is fixed at death.)

III. THE LAST WORDS, 38 C–42 A.

Little have you gained, Athenians, and great will be your loss. I could not have lived long, but now you will have the credit of having killed me. No defence but that which I adopted would have been worthy of myself. I have nothing to regret. It is my accusers who are the real sufferers.

Οὐ πολλοῦ γ' ἕνεκα χρόνου, ὦ ἄνδρες Ἀθηναῖοι, *(a) Address to the judges who had voted for his condemnation, 38 C–39 E.*
ὄνομα ἕξετε καὶ αἰτίαν ὑπὸ τῶν βουλομένων τὴν πόλιν
λοιδορεῖν, ὡς Σωκράτη ἀπεκτόνατε, ἄνδρα σοφόν·
φήσουσι γὰρ δή με σοφὸν εἶναι, εἰ καὶ μὴ εἰμί, οἱ
βουλόμενοι ὑμῖν ὀνειδίζειν. εἰ οὖν περιεμείνατε ὀλίγον
χρόνον, ἀπὸ τοῦ αὐτομάτου ἂν ὑμῖν τοῦτο ἐγένετο·
ὁρᾶτε γὰρ δὴ τὴν ἡλικίαν, ὅτι πόρρω ἤδη ἐστὶ τοῦ βίου,
θανάτου δὲ ἐγγύς. λέγω δὲ τοῦτο οὐ πρὸς πάντας ὑμᾶς,
D ἀλλὰ πρὸς τοὺς ἐμοῦ καταψηφισαμένους θάνατον. λέγω
δὲ καὶ τόδε πρὸς τοὺς αὐτοὺς τούτους. ἴσως με οἴεσθε,
ὦ ἄνδρες, ἀπορίᾳ λόγων ἑαλωκέναι τοιούτων, οἷς ἂν
ὑμᾶς ἔπεισα, εἰ ᾤμην δεῖν ἅπαντα ποιεῖν καὶ λέγειν,
ὥστε ἀποφυγεῖν τὴν δίκην. πολλοῦ γε δεῖ. ἀλλ' ἀπορίᾳ
μὲν ἑάλωκα, οὐ μέντοι λόγων, ἀλλὰ τόλμης καὶ ἀναι-
σχυντίας καὶ τοῦ ἐθέλειν λέγειν πρὸς ὑμᾶς τοιαῦτα, οἷ'
ἂν ὑμῖν ἥδιστ' ἦν ἀκούειν, θρηνοῦντός τέ μου καὶ ὀδυ-
E ρομένου καὶ ἄλλα ποιοῦντος καὶ λέγοντος πολλὰ καὶ

ἀνάξια ἐμοῦ, ὡς ἐγώ φημι· οἷα δὴ καὶ εἴθισθε ὑμεῖς τῶν ἄλλων ἀκούειν. ἀλλ' οὔτε τότε ᾠήθην δεῖν ἕνεκα τοῦ κινδύνου πρᾶξαι οὐδὲν ἀνελεύθερον, οὔτε νῦν μοι μεταμέλει οὕτως ἀπολογησαμένῳ, ἀλλὰ πολὺ μᾶλλον αἱροῦμαι ὧδε ἀπολογησάμενος τεθνάναι ἢ ἐκείνως ζῆν· οὔτε γὰρ ἐν δίκῃ οὔτ' ἐν πολέμῳ οὔτ' ἐμὲ οὔτ' ἄλλον οὐδένα δεῖ τοῦτο μηχανᾶσθαι, ὅπως ἀποφεύξεται πᾶν ποιῶν 39 θάνατον. καὶ γὰρ ἐν ταῖς μάχαις πολλάκις δῆλον γίγνεται ὅτι τό γε ἀποθανεῖν ἄν τις ἐκφύγοι καὶ ὅπλα ἀφεὶς καὶ ἐφ' ἱκετείαν τραπόμενος τῶν διωκόντων· καὶ ἄλλαι μηχαναὶ πολλαί εἰσιν ἐν ἑκάστοις τοῖς κινδύνοις, ὥστε διαφεύγειν θάνατον, ἐάν τις τολμᾷ πᾶν ποιεῖν καὶ λέγειν. ἀλλὰ μὴ οὐ τοῦτ' ᾖ χαλεπόν, ὦ ἄνδρες Ἀθηναῖοι, θάνατον ἐκφυγεῖν, ἀλλὰ πολὺ χαλεπώτερον πονηρίαν· θᾶττον γὰρ θανάτου θεῖ. καὶ νῦν ἐγὼ μὲν ἅτε βραδὺς ὢν καὶ πρεσ- B βύτης ὑπὸ τοῦ βραδυτέρου ἑάλων, οἱ δ' ἐμοὶ κατήγοροι ἅτε δεινοὶ καὶ ὀξεῖς ὄντες ὑπὸ τοῦ θάττονος, τῆς κακίας. καὶ νῦν ἐγὼ μὲν ἄπειμι ὑφ' ὑμῶν θανάτου δίκην ὀφλών, οὗτοι δ' ὑπὸ τῆς ἀληθείας ὠφληκότες μοχθηρίαν καὶ ἀδικίαν. καὶ ἐγώ τε τῷ τιμήματι ἐμμένω καὶ οὗτοι. ταῦτα μέν που ἴσως οὕτω καὶ ἔδει σχεῖν, καὶ οἶμαι αὐτὰ μετρίως ἔχειν.

Listen! For I am at the point when men are wont to prophesy. You will suffer for my condemnation. Others, whom I have held in check, will come forward to test your lives, and you will not be able to get rid of them.

Aprophecy. Τὸ δὲ δὴ μετὰ τοῦτο ἐπιθυμῶ ὑμῖν χρησμῳδῆσαι, ὦ καταψηφισάμενοί μου· καὶ γάρ εἰμι ἤδη ἐνταῦθα, C ἐν ᾧ μάλιστ' ἄνθρωποι χρησμῳδοῦσιν, ὅταν μέλλωσιν ἀποθανεῖσθαι. φημὶ γάρ, ὦ ἄνδρες, οἳ ἐμὲ ἀπεκτόνατε, τιμωρίαν ὑμῖν ἥξειν εὐθὺς μετὰ τὸν ἐμὸν θάνα-

τὸν πολὺ χαλεπωτέραν νὴ Δί᾽ ἢ οἵαν ἐμὲ ἀπεκτόνατε· νῦν γὰρ τοῦτο εἰργάσασθε οἰόμενοι ἀπαλλάξεσθαι τοῦ διδόναι ἔλεγχον τοῦ βίου, τὸ δὲ ὑμῖν πολὺ ἐναντίον ἀποβήσεται, ὡς ἐγώ φημι. πλείους ἔσονται ὑμᾶς οἱ D ἐλέγχοντες, οὓς νῦν ἐγὼ κατεῖχον, ὑμεῖς δὲ οὐκ ᾐσθάνεσθε· καὶ χαλεπώτεροι ἔσονται ὅσῳ νεώτεροί εἰσι, καὶ ὑμεῖς μᾶλλον ἀγανακτήσετε. εἰ γὰρ οἴεσθε ἀποκτείνοντες ἀνθρώπους ἐπισχήσειν τοῦ ὀνειδίζειν τινὰ ὑμῖν ὅτι οὐκ ὀρθῶς ζῆτε, οὐκ ὀρθῶς διανοεῖσθε· οὐ γάρ ἐσθ᾽ αὕτη ἡ ἀπαλλαγὴ οὔτε πάνυ δυνατὴ οὔτε καλή, ἀλλ᾽ ἐκείνη καὶ καλλίστη καὶ ῥᾴστη, μὴ τοὺς ἄλλους κολούειν, ἀλλ᾽ ἑαυτὸν παρασκευάζειν ὅπως ἔσται ὡς βέλτιστος. ταῦτα μὲν οὖν ὑμῖν τοῖς καταψηφισαμένοις μαντευσάμενος ἀπαλ-
E λάττομαι.

To you who have acquitted me I would fain say a few words, ere I go hence. I infer that death is no evil ; for the divine sign never came to hinder me throughout the whole course of the trial.

Τοῖς δὲ ἀποψηφισαμένοις ἡδέως ἂν διαλεχθείην ὑπὲρ τοῦ γεγονότος τουτουὶ πράγματος, ἐν ᾧ οἱ ἄρχοντες ἀσχολίαν ἄγουσι καὶ οὔπω ἔρχομαι οἷ ἐλθόντα με δεῖ τεθνάναι. ἀλλά μοι, ὦ ἄνδρες, παραμείνατε τοσοῦτον χρόνον· οὐδὲν γὰρ κωλύει διαμυθολογῆσαι πρὸς ἀλλή-
40 λους, ἕως ἔξεστιν. ὑμῖν γὰρ ὡς φίλοις οὖσιν ἐπιδεῖξαι ἐθέλω τὸ νυνί μοι ξυμβεβηκὸς τί ποτε νοεῖ. ἐμοὶ γάρ, ὦ ἄνδρες δικασταί — ὑμᾶς γὰρ δικαστὰς καλῶν ὀρθῶς ἂν καλοίην — θαυμάσιόν τι γέγονεν. ἡ γὰρ εἰωθυῖά μοι μαντικὴ ἡ τοῦ δαιμονίου ἐν μὲν τῷ πρόσθεν χρόνῳ παντὶ πάνυ πυκνὴ ἀεὶ ἦν καὶ πάνυ ἐπὶ σμικροῖς ἐναντιουμένη, εἴ τι μέλλοιμι μὴ ὀρθῶς πράξειν· νυνὶ δὲ ξυμβέβηκέ μοι, ἅπερ ὁρᾶτε καὶ αὐτοί, ταυτί, ἅ γε δὴ οἰηθείη ἄν τις καὶ
E

(*b*) Address to the judges who had voted for his acquittal, 39 E-42 A

νομίζεται ἔσχατα κακῶν εἶναι. ἐμοὶ δὲ οὔτε ἐξιόντι ἕωθεν οἴκοθεν ἠναντιώθη τὸ τοῦ θεοῦ σημεῖον, οὔτε ἡνίκα ἀνέ- B βαινον ἐνταυθοῖ [ἐπὶ τὸ δικαστήριον], οὔτ' ἐν τῷ λόγῳ οὐδαμοῦ μέλλοντί τι ἐρεῖν· καίτοι ἐν ἄλλοις λόγοις πολλαχοῦ δή με ἐπέσχε λέγοντα μεταξύ· νυνὶ δὲ οὐδαμοῦ περὶ ταύτην τὴν πρᾶξιν οὔτ' ἐν ἔργῳ οὐδενὶ οὔτ' ἐν λόγῳ ἠναντίωταί μοι. τί οὖν αἴτιον εἶναι ὑπολαμβάνω; ἐγὼ ὑμῖν ἐρῶ· κινδυνεύει γάρ μοι τὸ ξυμβεβηκὸς τοῦτο ἀγαθὸν γεγονέναι, καὶ οὐκ ἔσθ' ὅπως ἡμεῖς ὀρθῶς ὑπολαμβάνομεν, ὅσοι οἰόμεθα κακὸν εἶναι τὸ τεθνάναι. μέγα C μοι τεκμήριον τούτου γέγονεν· οὐ γὰρ ἔσθ' ὅπως οὐκ ἠναντιώθη ἄν μοι τὸ εἰωθὸς σημεῖον, εἰ μή τι ἔμελλον ἐγὼ ἀγαθὸν πράξειν.

Nay, there is much reason to hope that death is actually a good. For death is either a dreamless sleep, which is better than the average experiences of life, or else it is a migration to a place where we shall be able to meet and converse with the famous dead—and what can be better than this?

Death either annihilation or a happy change.

Ἐννοήσωμεν δὲ καὶ τῇδε, ὡς πολλὴ ἐλπίς ἐστιν ἀγαθὸν αὐτὸ εἶναι. δυοῖν γὰρ θάτερόν ἐστι τὸ τεθνάναι· ἢ γὰρ οἷον μηδὲν εἶναι μηδ' αἴσθησιν μηδεμίαν μηδενὸς ἔχειν τὸν τεθνεῶτα, ἢ κατὰ τὰ λεγόμενα μεταβολή τις τυγχάνει οὖσα καὶ μετοίκησις τῇ ψυχῇ τοῦ τόπου τοῦ ἐνθένδε εἰς ἄλλον τόπον. καὶ εἴτε μηδεμία αἴσθησίς ἐστιν, ἀλλ' οἷον ὕπνος, ἐπειδάν τις D καθεύδων μηδ' ὄναρ μηδὲν ὁρᾷ, θαυμάσιον κέρδος ἂν εἴη ὁ θάνατος. ἐγὼ γὰρ ἂν οἶμαι, εἴ τινα ἐκλεξάμενον δέοι ταύτην τὴν νύκτα, ἐν ᾗ οὕτω κατέδαρθεν, ὥστε μηδ' ὄναρ ἰδεῖν, καὶ τὰς ἄλλας νύκτας τε καὶ ἡμέρας τὰς τοῦ βίου τοῦ ἑαυτοῦ ἀντιπαραθέντα ταύτῃ τῇ νυκτὶ δέοι σκεψάμενον εἰπεῖν, πόσας ἄμεινον καὶ ἥδιον ἡμέρας

καὶ νύκτας ταύτης τῆς νυκτὸς βεβίωκεν ἐν τῷ ἑαυτοῦ βίῳ,
E οἶμαι ἂν μὴ ὅτι ἰδιώτην τινά, ἀλλὰ τὸν μέγαν βασιλέα εὐαριθμήτους ἂν εὑρεῖν αὐτὸν ταύτας πρὸς τὰς ἄλλας ἡμέρας καὶ νύκτας. εἰ οὖν τοιοῦτον ὁ θάνατός ἐστι, κέρδος ἔγωγε λέγω· καὶ γὰρ οὐδὲν πλείων ὁ πᾶς χρόνος φαίνεται οὕτω δὴ εἶναι ἢ μία νύξ. εἰ δ' αὖ οἷον ἀποδημῆσαί ἐστιν ὁ θάνατος ἐνθένδε εἰς ἄλλον τόπον, καὶ ἀληθῆ ἐστὶ τὰ λεγόμενα, ὡς ἄρα ἐκεῖ εἰσὶν ἅπαντες οἱ τεθνεῶτες, τί μεῖζον ἀγαθὸν τούτου εἴη ἄν, ὦ ἄνδρες δικασταί; εἰ γάρ
41 τις ἀφικόμενος εἰς Ἅιδου, ἀπαλλαγεὶς τούτων τῶν φασκόν-   The judges των δικαστῶν εἶναι, εὑρήσει τοὺς ἀληθῶς δικαστάς, οἵπερ   in the other world. καὶ λέγονται ἐκεῖ δικάζειν, Μίνως τε καὶ Ῥαδάμανθυς καὶ Αἰακὸς καὶ Τριπτόλεμος καὶ ἄλλοι ὅσοι τῶν ἡμιθέων δίκαιοι ἐγένοντο ἐν τῷ ἑαυτῶν βίῳ, ἆρα φαύλη ἂν εἴη ἡ ἀποδημία; ἢ αὖ Ὀρφεῖ ξυγγενέσθαι καὶ Μουσαίῳ   The poets. καὶ Ἡσιόδῳ καὶ Ὁμήρῳ ἐπὶ πόσῳ ἄν τις δέξαιτ' ἂν ὑμῶν; ἐγὼ μὲν γὰρ πολλάκις ἐθέλω τεθνάναι, εἰ ταῦτ' ἐστὶν ἀληθῆ· ἐπεὶ ἔμοιγε καὶ αὐτῷ θαυμαστὴ ἂν
B εἴη ἡ διατριβὴ αὐτόθι, ὁπότε ἐντύχοιμι Παλαμήδει καὶ   Palamedes and Ajax. Αἴαντι τῷ Τελαμῶνος καὶ εἴ τις ἄλλος τῶν παλαιῶν διὰ κρίσιν ἄδικον τέθνηκεν, ἀντιπαραβάλλοντι τὰ ἐμαυτοῦ πάθη πρὸς τὰ ἐκείνων, ὡς ἐγὼ οἶμαι, οὐκ ἂν ἀηδὲς εἴη. καὶ δὴ τὸ μέγιστον, τοὺς ἐκεῖ ἐξετάζοντα καὶ ἐρευνῶντα ὥσπερ τοὺς ἐνταῦθα διάγειν, τίς αὐτῶν σοφός ἐστι καὶ τίς οἴεται μέν, ἔστι δ' οὔ. ἐπὶ πόσῳ δ' ἄν τις, ὦ ἄνδρες δικασταί, δέξαιτο ἐξετάσαι τὸν ἐπὶ Τροίαν ἀγαγόντα τὴν πολλὴν στρατιὰν ἢ Ὀδυσσέα ἢ   Ulysses and Sisyphus.
C Σίσυφον, ἢ ἄλλους μυρίους ἄν τις εἴποι καὶ ἄνδρας καὶ γυναῖκας; οἷς ἐκεῖ διαλέγεσθαι καὶ ξυνεῖναι καὶ ἐξετάζειν ἀμήχανον ἂν εἴη εὐδαιμονίας. πάντως οὐ δήπου τούτου γε ἕνεκα οἱ ἐκεῖ ἀποκτείνουσι· τά τε γὰρ ἄλλα

εὐδαιμονέστεροί εἰσιν οἱ ἐκεῖ τῶν ἐνθάδε, καὶ ἤδη τὸν λοιπὸν χρόνον ἀθάνατοί εἰσιν, εἴπερ γε τὰ λεγόμενα ἀληθῆ ἐστίν.

One thing is certain. No evil can happen to a good man in this world or the next. What has befallen me has not taken place without the divine sanction; and I bear no ill-will against my accusers. Only I beg of them to deal with my sons as faithfully as I have dealt with them. And now we part on our several ways — which is the better, God only knows.

Ἀλλὰ καὶ ὑμᾶς χρή, ὦ ἄνδρες δικασταί, εὐέλπιδας εἶναι πρὸς τὸν θάνατον, καὶ ἕν τι τοῦτο διανοεῖσθαι ἀληθές, ὅτι οὐκ ἔστιν ἀνδρὶ ἀγαθῷ κακὸν οὐδὲν οὔτε D ζῶντι οὔτε τελευτήσαντι, οὐδὲ ἀμελεῖται ὑπὸ θεῶν τὰ τούτου πράγματα· οὐδὲ τὰ ἐμὰ νῦν ἀπὸ τοῦ αὐτομάτου γέγονεν, ἀλλά μοι δῆλόν ἐστι τοῦτο, ὅτι ἤδη τεθνάναι καὶ ἀπηλλάχθαι πραγμάτων βέλτιον ἦν μοι. διὰ τοῦτο καὶ ἐμὲ οὐδαμοῦ ἀπέτρεψε τὸ σημεῖον, καὶ ἔγωγε τοῖς καταψηφισαμένοις μου καὶ τοῖς κατηγόροις οὐ πάνυ χαλεπαίνω. καίτοι οὐ ταύτῃ τῇ διανοίᾳ κατεψηφίζοντό μου καὶ κατηγόρουν, ἀλλ' οἰόμενοι βλάπτειν· τοῦτο αὐτοῖς ἄξιον μέμφεσθαι. τοσόνδε μέντοι αὐτῶν δέομαι· E τοὺς υἱεῖς μου, ἐπειδὰν ἡβήσωσι, τιμωρήσασθε, ὦ ἄνδρες, ταὐτὰ ταῦτα λυποῦντες, ἅπερ ἐγὼ ὑμᾶς ἐλύπουν, ἐὰν ὑμῖν δοκῶσιν ἢ χρημάτων ἢ ἄλλου του πρότερον ἐπιμελεῖσθαι ἢ ἀρετῆς, καὶ ἐὰν δοκῶσί τι εἶναι μηδὲν ὄντες, ὀνειδίζετε αὐτοῖς, ὥσπερ ἐγὼ ὑμῖν, ὅτι οὐκ ἐπιμελοῦνται ὧν δεῖ, καὶ οἴονταί τι εἶναι ὄντες οὐδενὸς ἄξιοι. καὶ ἐὰν ταῦτα 42 ποιῆτε, δίκαια πεπονθὼς ἐγὼ ἔσομαι ὑφ' ὑμῶν αὐτός τε καὶ οἱ υἱεῖς. ἀλλὰ γὰρ ἤδη ὥρα ἀπιέναι, ἐμοὶ μὲν ἀποθανουμένῳ, ὑμῖν δὲ βιωσομένοις· ὁπότεροι δὲ ἡμῶν ἔρχονται ἐπὶ ἄμεινον πρᾶγμα, ἄδηλον παντὶ πλὴν ἢ τῷ θεῷ.

Last charge to the condemning jurors.

Clarendon Press Series

THE
APOLOGY OF PLATO

WITH INTRODUCTION AND NOTES

BY

ST GEORGE STOCK, M.A.

PEMBROKE COLLEGE

THIRD EDITION, REVISED

PART II—NOTES

Oxford

AT THE CLARENDON PRESS

1899

NOTES.

πεπόνθατε ὑπό] 'Have been affected by.' πάσχειν is in effect a **17 A** passive verb, and is regularly constructed as such. See for instance 33 D, 42 A The same is the case with ὀφλισκάνω (see 39 B, ὑφ' ὑμῶν θανάτου δίκην ὄφλων) and with φεύγω (see 35 D, ἀσεβείας φεύγοντα ὑπὸ Μελήτου τουτουί).

ὑπ' αὐτῶν] 'By reason of them,' 'under their influence.' For this use of ὑπό cp Gorg. 525 A, καὶ πάντα σκολιὰ ὑπὸ ψεύδους; also Ion 535 E

ὀλίγου] 'Almost' Cp. 22 B; Prot 361 C, ὀλίγου πάντα μᾶλλον φανῆναι αὐτὸ ἢ ἐπιστήμην.

ὡς ἔπος εἰπεῖν] 'To put it roughly' One of the many modes which Attic politeness prompted of apologizing for a strong assertion. Cp 22 B, D

αὐτῶν] 'In them' Cp below, B, τοῦτό μοι ἔδοξεν αὐτῶν ἀναισχυντότατον εἶναι The construction θαυμάζειν τί τινος is common in Plato, e. g Theaet. 161 B, ὃ θαυμάζω τοῦ ἑταίρου σου.

τοῦτο ἐν ᾧ ἔλεγον] 'The passage in which they said.'

δεινοῦ ὄντος λέγειν] Cp what Xenophon says (Mem I. 2. § 14) about Socrates twisting everyone round his finger in discussion Socrates, like Berkeley, had the reputation of being invincible in argument

χρή] In indirect quotations after ὅτι and ὡς, the tense of the direct discourse is always retained in the indirect. The mood also is always retained after primary, and may be retained after historical tenses; otherwise it is changed into the optative, so that we might here have χρείη. See Goodwin, Moods and Tenses, § 69. It follows that the reading χρῆν, which is supported by good MSS, is not the indirect equivalent of χρή, but would imply a belief on the part of the speakers that the judges were not likely to exercise due caution.

ἔργῳ] 'In the most practical way' There is a suppressed **B** antithesis of λόγῳ.

εἰ μέν] Here we have an instance of the use of μέν without any contrasted clause following. Cp. 26 E; Meno 82 B, 89 C. We have it also in the often-recurring phrase πάνυ μὲν οὖν, for which see especially Xen Conv. IV. §§ 56-62.

οὐ κατὰ τούτους εἶναι ῥήτωρ] 'That I am a far greater orator than they.' This is an instance of the figure *meiosis* or *litotes*, which consists in saying less than is meant. It abounds in Plato, being characteristic of the εἰρωνεία of Socrates. For the special use of κατά in the sense of 'on a level with,' cp Gorg. 512 B, μή σοι δοκεῖ (ὁ μηχανοποιὸς) κατὰ τὸν δικανικὸν εἶναι ;

ἤ τι ἢ οὐδὲν ἀληθές] 'Little or nothing that is true.'

μὰ Δί'] The accusative after adverbs of swearing is a use which it would not be easy to classify. Notice that νή is used in affirmative, but μά in negative oaths, except where ναί precedes it

ῥήμασί τε καὶ ὀνόμασιν] 'Expressions and words.' The distinction between these two terms is a somewhat fluctuating one. In the Cratylus (399 A, B) we are told that Διὶ φίλος is a ῥῆμα, but that the omission of one of the iotas and the suppression of the acute accent in the middle converts it into an ὄνομα, Δίφιλος. In the strict grammatical sense ὄνομα and ῥῆμα are the two parts of which a λόγος or proposition consists, ὄνομα being noun and ῥῆμα verb. Plato gives as instances of ὀνόματα—λέων, ἔλαφος, ἵππος, and as instances of ῥήματα—βαδίζει, τρέχει, καθεύδει. The λόγος in its simplest form consists of the combination of one ὄνομα and one ῥῆμα, as ἄνθρωπος μανθάνει. Soph 262 A-C.

C τῇδε τῇ ἡλικίᾳ] 'To a man of my years.' The three demonstrative pronouns, ὅδε, οὗτος and ἐκεῖνος, with their derivatives correspond roughly to the three personal pronouns, με, σε, ἑ. Thus below, 18 C. it is ταύτῃ τῇ ἡλικίᾳ, where the persons addressed are meant

παρίεμαι] 'Crave indulgence.' παρίεσθαι has the meaning of 'to beg to be let off.' Cp. Rep 341 C, οὐδέν σου παρίεμαι, 'I ask no quarter'

ἐπὶ τῶν τραπεζῶν] 'At the counters.' τράπεζα was specially used of the table of a money-dealer, and hence came to mean a bank, and τραπεζίτης a banker, as in the speech of Demosthenes against Phormio. Cp. Matt. xxi. 12 ; Mark xi 15 ; John ii 15—τὰς τραπέζας τῶν κολλυβιστῶν. The money-changer sitting at his table in the market-place is still a familiar sight in the smaller towns of the east of Europe. To discourse 'at the counters in the market-place' was not peculiar to Socrates. Hipp Min. 368 B.

D μήτε θαυμάζειν κ.τ λ] This is epexegetical. i. e. explanatory, of the τοῦτο after δέομαι καὶ παρίεμαι.

νῦν ἐγὼ πρῶτον] This, as the Scholiast remarks, has the force of an objection to the indictment, since Socrates' mode of life had escaped censure for so many years

ἀναβέβηκα] 'Presented myself before a court.' The ἀνά refers to mounting the βῆμα, or raised platform from which the speeches were delivered. Cp 31 C. 33 D, 36 A, 40 B. Similarly with ἀναβιβάζομαι, 34 C, D. As a rule accusers are said εἰσάγειν, defendants εἰσιέναι. Speakers are said ἀναβαίνειν (to step up), καταβαίνειν (to step down).

ἔτη γεγονὼς ἑβδομήκοντα] In the Crito, 52 E, Socrates is made to talk of himself as being 70 years old. According to the statement of Apollodorus, confirmed by Demetrius Phalereus (Diog. Laert. II § 44) Socrates was born in the 4th year of the 77th Olympiad, and died in the first year of the 95th Olympiad. The date of the first Olympiad being B.C. 776, this corresponds to B.C. 468–399, which would make Socrates 69 at the time of his death. Another reading is πλείω ἑβδομήκοντα, which cannot be accepted, unless we place the birth of Socrates a few years earlier than is done by Apollodorus.

δίκαιον] 'As a piece of justice' Riddell.

αὕτη ἀρετή] ἀρετή is shown to be predicate by the omission of the article. The subject αὕτη is attracted into its gender.

δίκαιός εἰμι ἀπολογήσασθαι] 'It is right that I should make my defence.' By a common Greek idiom that is expressed personally which, in Latin or English, would be expressed impersonally. Instances abound, e.g. Crito 45 A ad in., Gorg. 461 D, 521 A; Menex 237 D, δικαία ἐπαινεῖσθαι, 246 C, δίκαιός εἰμι εἰπεῖν. Demosthenes against Aristocrates, p. 641, § 64, Dindorf) furnishes us with a strong example, ἆ . . . ἡδίους ἔσεσθε ἀκούσαντες. We may compare the preference of the Greek for personal forms of expression in such phrases as τυγχάνω ὤν, φαίνομαι ὤν, etc.

ἐμοῦ] The genitive is governed by the verbal notion contained in κατήγοροι.

καὶ πάλαι κ.τ.λ.] The καί merely emphasizes the πάλαι, of which πολλὰ ἤδη ἔτη is epexegetical. The words πολλὰ ἤδη ἔτη seem to come under the government of λέγοντες as an accusative of duration of time.

It was 24 years since the first representation of the Clouds of Aristophanes (B.C. 423).

τοὺς ἀμφὶ Ἄνυτον] 'Anytus and his coadjutors.' This form of expression includes as the principal the person whose name is mentioned. It is as old as Homer. See for instance Il. IV 252. Cp. Meno 99 B, οἱ ἀμφὶ Θεμιστοκλέα, 'Themistocles and the like.' Anytus was by far the most important of the three accusers of Socrates. Hence the 'Anytique reum' of Horace (Sat II. iv. 3). See note on 23 E, Ἄνυτος.

μᾶλλον οὐδὲν ἀληθές] 'Were more busy in trying to persuade you and in accusing me.' The μᾶλλον implies that the greater urgency of the former set of accusers was a reason for their being more formidable. In Hermann's edition these words are placed in brackets.

τά τε μετέωρα] The accusative is governed by the verbal substantive φροντιστής. So in Latin, Plaut. Aul 420, 'sed quid tibi nos tactiost?' Caesar, Bell. Gall I 5, 'domum reditionis.' For the subject-matter see notes on 19 B, C.

C **οἱ γὰρ ἀκούοντες κ.τ λ.**] Here we have in an early stage the antagonism between science and theology—between the science which looks only at physical causes and the theology which delights to trace the action of Deity in aberration from general law.

οὐδὲ θεοὺς νομίζειν] 'Do not even believe in gods' So below 24 B, 35 D; Prot. 322 A, ὁ ἄνθρωπος . . . ζῴων μόνον θεοὺς ἐνόμισε, with which cp. Menex 237 D This use of νομίζειν is very common. ἡγεῖσθαι is employed in a similar way. See below 27 D, E, 35 D; and cp. Eur Hec. 800,

νύμῳ γὰρ τοὺς θεοὺς ἡγούμεθα.

ἔνιοι δ' ὑμῶν καὶ μειράκια] This clause is thrown in parenthetically to correct the preceding one, παῖδες ὄντες. 'When you were children—though some of you may have been striplings'

ἐρήμην] Supply δίκην, which is cognate to κατηγοροῦντες ἐρήμη δίκη is a technical term for a suit which goes by default owing to the non appearance of one of the parties.

ὃ δὲ πάντων ἀλογώτατον] Riddell fills up the construction thus —ὁ δὲ πάντων ἐστὶν ἀλογώτατον, ἐστὶ τοῦτο κ τ λ

D **πλὴν εἴ τις**] Like Latin *nisi si quis*. Εἴ τις is 'anyone who,' εἴ τι, 'anything which,' etc

κωμῳδιοποιός] Notably Aristophanes in the Clouds Eupolis also had ridiculed him as a beggarly gossip:—

Μισῶ δ' ἐγὼ καὶ Σωκράτην, τὸν πτωχὸν ἀδολέσχην
ὃς τἆλλα μὲν πεφρόντικεν,
ὁπόθεν δὲ καταφαγεῖν ἔχοι, τούτου κατημέληκεν.

(Meineke vol. II. p. 553, Berlin, 1839). The Connus of Ameipsias too, which was represented along with the Clouds, may have contained ridicule of Socrates; for the chorus was of Phrontistae (Athen. 218 C, and Connus, the son of Metrobius is represented as having taught Socrates music in his old age (Euthyd. 272 C, Menex 235 E). See Meineke vol. I. p. 203. We may add that Ameipsias certainly held up Socrates to ridicule in his play of the Τρίβων or Old Cloak (Diog Laert. II. § 48):—

Σώκρατες, ἀνδρῶν βέλτιστ' ὀλίγων, πολλῶν δὲ ματαιόταθ', ἥκεις
καὶ σὺ πρὸς ἡμᾶς, καρτερικός τ' εἶ. Πόθεν ἄν σοι χλαῖνα γένοιτο;
τουτὶ τὸ κακὸν τῶν σκυτοτόμων κατ' ἐπήρειαν γεγένηται.

APOLOGY, NOTES. 18 D–19 B.

οἱ δὲ καὶ αὐτοί κ.τ.λ.] A parenthetical clause corrective of the preceding, like the one noticed above, 18 C, ἔνιοι δ' ὑμῶν κ.τ.λ. Translate, 'though some of them may have been convinced themselves when they tried to convince others.'

ἀλλ' ἀνάγκη κ.τ λ] 'But one has absolutely to fight with shadows, as it were, in conducting his defence and cross-questioning.'

καὶ γὰρ ὑμεῖς] 'For you also.' The καί has here its full force, so that the expression is equivalent to καὶ γὰρ καί. Cp. Meno 97 E, καὶ γὰρ αἱ δόξαι κ τ.λ.

πολὺ μᾶλλον] Supply ἠκούσατε κατηγορούντων.

διαβολήν 'Calumny believed, i. e. prejudice' Riddell. Cp. 28 19 A A, and 37 B.

ἐξελέσθαι . χρόνῳ] 'To disabuse your minds in so short a time of this prejudice which you have had so long to acquire' The aorist ἔσχετε belongs to the class which is known as 'aorist of first attainment,' like ἐβασίλευσε, 'he became king,' ἦρξε, 'he began to reign' We have the perfect ἔσχηκα in the same sense below, 20 D.

εἴ τι ἄμεινον] Supply εἴη.

καὶ οὐ πάνυ κ.τ.λ] 'And am far from being deceived as to the nature of it.' Οὐ πάνυ often practically has the meaning of 'not at all,' *omnino non*, but this is arrived at by an ironical *litotes*, as its literal meaning is always *non omnino*, 'not quite,' 'not much,' 'hardly,' etc. See the subject exhaustively discussed in Appendix, note C, to Cope's translation of the Gorgias; see also Riddell, Digest § 139, and Thompson, Gorgias, note on 457 E. The passages cited by the last-mentioned writer in favour of taking οὐ πάνυ as an unqualified negation seem to lend themselves readily to the other interpretation, e. g. the passage quoted from Aristotle, Eth Nic. X. (5). § 4, χαίροντες ὁτῳοῦν σφόδρα οὐ πάνυ δρῶμεν ἕτερον, 'we are remiss in doing anything else.' The strongest of them is Laws 704 C, where οὐ πάνυ is used in answer to a question, to convey an emphatic denial; but even this is sufficiently accounted for by the inveterate εἰρωνεία of the Attic diction.

τῷ θεῷ] We may render this simply 'God.' There has been no reference to Apollo or any special deity

Μέλητος] The son of Meletus and a member of the deme Pitthis (Diog Laert. II § 40). He is referred to in the Euthyphro, 2 B, as a young and obscure man; and is described as having long straight hair, not much beard, and a hooked nose. The Scholiast informs us that he was a bad tragic poet, and a Thracian by extraction. We learn from 23 E that he posed as the representative of the poets in the attack on Socrates. Six years before this date, at the time when the Frogs was produced (B.C. 405), a poet named Meletus possessed notoriety enough to attract the attacks of Aristophanes. In that play Aeschylus is made to charge Euripides with imitating the σκόλια of Meletus (Frogs 1302, Dindorf) Meletus also, we are told, was mentioned by Aristophanes in the Γεωργοί, which is known to have been represented considerably earlier Unless Plato has greatly exaggerated the youth and obscurity of Meletus, we may suppose the poet referred to by Aristophanes to have been the father of Socrates' accuser This would account sufficiently for his taking up the quarrel of the poets One of the four men who arrested Leon of Salamis (see below 32 C), was named Meletus (Andocides, de Mysteriis, § 94) Diogenes Laertius (II. § 43), declares that when the Athenians repented of their treatment of Socrates, they condemned Meletus to death. Diodorus (XIV. 37 ad fin.) goes so far as to say that the accusers were executed in a body But there is no valid evidence to show that this change of sentiment ever really occurred in the minds of the generation which condemned Socrates Had any untoward fate befallen Anytus, it could not fail to have been mentioned in Xenophon's Apologia (§ 31), which was written after his death. The name is variously spelt Μέλητος and Μέλιτος. This is part of that confusion known among scholars by the term 'itacism' Whatever may have been the case in ancient times, the vowels η, ι, υ and diphthongs ει, οι have now all precisely the same sound in Greek, namely that of the English long *e*. See Thompson's Gorgias, p 80.

διέβαλλον οἱ διαβάλλοντες] The fulness of expression gives an air of deliberation, Riddell, Digest, § 262, 3 Cp Crito 48 A, ὥστε πρῶτον μὲν ταύτῃ οὐκ ὀρθῶς εἰσηγεῖ, εἰσηγούμενος κ.τ.λ.

ἀντωμοσίαν] 'Affidavit' Cp. 24 B, τὴν τούτων ἀντωμοσίαν There was much uncertainty among the Ancients themselves as to the proper meaning of this term. According to the Scholiast on this passage ἀντωμοσία was used of the counter-oaths taken by the prosecutor and defendant at the beginning of a suit, the one swearing that a wrong had been committed, the other that it had not He mentions another view, that ἀντωμοσία properly referred to the defendant's oath only, while διωμοσία was the name for the oath taken by the prosecutor The following is the result which Meier and Schomann have arrived at from a thorough examination of the whole question (Der Attische Process, pp. 624, 625, edit. of 1824): 'The prosecutor's oath, according to the grammarians, is properly called προωμοσία, that of the defendant ἀντωμοσία. both together διωμοσία Still the word ἀντωμοσία is often used for both (i. e. singly as well as together, as the examples selected show), and διωμοσία denotes not merely both together, but often one of the two' It is plain that in the present passage ἀντωμοσία is neither more nor less than 'indictment,' the proper term for which is ἔγκλημα, which we have in 24 C ad in. The word is explained by Plato himself in the Theaetetus, 172 D, E: κατεπείγει γὰρ ὕδωρ ῥέον, καὶ οὐκ ἐγχωρεῖ περὶ οὗ ἂν ἐπιθυμήσωσι τοὺς λόγους ποιεῖσθαι, ἀλλ' ἀνάγκην ἔχων ὁ ἀντίδικος ἐφέστηκε καὶ ὑπογραφὴν παραναγιγνωσκομένην, ὧν ἐκτὸς οὐ ῥητέον· ἣν ἀντωμοσίαν καλοῦσιν. Here we see that ἀντωμοσία was understood by Plato to mean the written statement on oath of the points in dispute between two litigants.

ἀναγνῶναι] This word, like *recitare* in Latin, often means to read out. Hence ἀναγνώστης, a trained reader (Cic. ad Att. I 12 ad fin.; Corn. Nep. Att 13).

Σωκράτης ἀδικεῖ κ.τ.λ.] This is a parody on the real indictment, which began with the same words. See 24 B ad fin. This mock indictment shows us plainly the way in which Socrates' character was misconceived by his countrymen. He was regarded with suspicion as a physical philosopher with atheistical proclivities and as an unscrupulous sophist who subordinated truth to cleverness

περιεργάζεται] 'Follows curious inquiries.' So Purves, who compares the use of the adjective in Acts xix. 19, ἱκανοὶ δὲ τῶν τὰ περίεργα πραξάντων. The transition of thought from physical science to magic is very easy to the uneducated. We have a parody on the 'curious inquiries' which were supposed to occupy the mind of Socrates in the philosopher's experiment to ascertain how many times the length of its own foot a flea could jump (Arist. Clouds 144-152).

τῇ Ἀριστοφάνους κωμῳδίᾳ] The Clouds. For searching into things beneath the earth and things in heaven, see the broad burlesque in 187-201, and for making the worse appear the better cause, see especially 112-18, and the dialogue between the two λόγοι, 886-1104.

περιφερόμενον] Socrates is represented on the stage in a swing (line 218):

φέρε τίς γὰρ οὗτος οὑπὶ τῆς κρεμάθρας ἀνήρ;

ἀεροβατεῖν] Socrates, when asked by Strepsiades what he is doing up in the basket, replies (line 225).—

ἀεροβατῶ καὶ περιφρονῶ τὸν ἥλιον

'My feet are on the air,
My thoughts are in the sun.'—E. A.

ὧν ἐγὼ οὐδέν] Xenophon represents Socrates as having an aversion from physical speculations on the ground of their utter impracticability and remoteness from human interests (Mem. I. 1. §§ 11-15). On the limits of the profitable study of science as conceived of by Socrates see Mem. IV. 7. §§ 2-8.

μή πως ἐγώ κ.τ.λ.] 'I hope to goodness I may not be prosecuted by Meletus upon so grave a charge' It is not necessary to take τοσαῦτας of number, = *tot*. The use of the plural for the singular in the phrase δίκας φεύγειν is well borne out by a number of similar phrases which are collected by Liddell and Scott, sub voce IV. 3. The words are a mere passing gibe. 'I had better mind what I'm saying, for there is no knowing for what Meletus may fall foul of me'

ἀλλὰ γάρ] 'But indeed.' This idiom is of specially frequent occurrence in the Apology, perhaps because the diction is designedly colloquial. Cp. below D ad fin., 20 C ad in., 25 C ad in., also Meno 92 C, 94 E The idiom is as old as Homer, and may always be explained by the theory of an ellipse of some kind after the ἀλλά See, for instance, Od. X. 201, 2—

κλαῖον δὲ λιγέως, θαλερὸν κατὰ δάκρυ χέοντες·
ἀλλ' οὐ γάρ τις πρῆξις ἐγίγνετο μυρομένοισι,

where Merry supplies the ellipse thus: 'but [all in vain] for no good came by their weeping.' Shilleto, however, maintains, in his note to Thucydides, Bk. I. ch. 25, that in this use of γάρ we have a relic of an original meaning 'truly,' 'verily,' parallel to that of the Latin *nam* and *enim*. In that case we may compare ἀλλὰ γάρ with the use of *sed enim* in Virgil, Aen I. 19—

'Progeniem sed enim Troiano a sanguine duci
Audierat.'

D ἔστιν] 'Is so,' i. e. as alleged. Cp. Acts xxv. 11, εἰ δὲ οὐδέν ἐστιν ὧν οὗτοι κατηγοροῦσί μου

E χρήματα πράττομαι] This implication pervades the Clouds. See especially line 98—

οὗτοι διδάσκουσ', ἀργύριον ἤν τις διδῷ.

That Socrates never taught for money is abundantly evident from the express testimony of his disciples. Cp. below 31 B, C, and see note on 33 A, οὐδὲ χρήματα μὲν λαμβάνων κ.τ λ. Aristoxenus, however, a disciple of Aristotle, who wrote a life of Socrates, is quoted by Diogenes Laertius (II § 20) as recording that Socrates from time to time collected voluntary contributions—τιθέντα γοῦν, τὸ βαλλόμενον κέρμα ἀθροίζειν εἶτ' ἀναλώσαντα, πάλιν τιθέναι. τιθέντα evidently refers to some kind of subscription-box The invidious word, χρηματίσασθαι, which precedes is probably due to Diogenes himself, who delights in a bit of scandal. This story has been summarily rejected even by those who accept the general testimony of Aristoxenus as trustworthy; but there is, after all, nothing improbable in the statement that Socrates allowed his friends to help him, nor anything inconsistent with the professions which are put into his mouth by his disciples. The reasons on which Socrates rested his violent antipathy to teaching virtue for money are (1) that it was degrading, as the teacher made himself for the time being the slave of the man from whom he was expecting a fee, and (2) that it involved an absurdity, as, if moral benefit were really imparted, the person so improved would be anxious to display his gratitude On this subject cp. Xen. Mem. I. 2. § 7 with Gorg. 520 E, where the following test is laid down of such teaching being effectual, ὥστε καλὸν δοκεῖ τὸ σημεῖον εἶναι, εἰ εὖ ποιήσας ταύτην τὴν εὐεργεσίαν ἀντ' εὖ πείσεται. Human beings, even the most exalted, must live somehow. Socrates had no private property, and did not work for his living. We are therefore driven to the conclusion that he was supported by voluntary contributions. See Xen. Œc. II. § 8

ἐπεί] This use of ἐπεί points to an ellipse before it. (Not that I mean to disparage those who do undertake to educate people) since, etc ἐπεί, when used thus, may be rendered ' though.'

Γοργίας] A celebrated rhetorician, a native of Leontium in Sicily He was an elder contemporary of Socrates, but is said to have outlived him (Quint. III 1. § 9). We are told that he attained to an enormous age. It is put by Cicero at 107. See De Senectute, ch. 5, where we are informed that his most celebrated pupil, Isocrates, died at the age of 99

The dialogue of Plato which goes under the name of Gorgias begins with a discussion on the meaning and power of rhetoric, but ends with an earnest vindication of the life of virtue against the corrupt political tendencies of the times

Πρόδικος] A native of the island of Ceos, and one of the most popular ' teachers of virtue ' of his day. He is best known now as the original author of the charming allegory called the ' Choice of Hercules,' which is preserved in Xenophon's Memorabilia (II. 1 §§ 21-34). This piece was an ἐπίδειξις, or show-speech (ὅπερ δὴ καὶ πλείστοις ἐπιδείκνυται, ibid. § 21. Cp. Plato Crat 384 B, τὴν πεντηκοντάδραχμον ἐπίδειξιν; Gorg. 447 C; Hipp. Maj. 282 B, C). The Choice of Hercules shines out like a gem amid its somewhat dull surroundings; one can feel the impress of a master-mind in the picturesqueness of its imagery: but Xenophon modestly declares that it fell from the lips of the author in far more magnificent phraseology than that in which he has clothed it. Prodicus had a peculiarly deep voice, which rendered his utterance indistinct (δυσήκοον καὶ βαρὺ φθεγγόμενος, Philostratus, Lives of the Sophists, p. 210). Cp. Prot. 316 A ad in.

Ἱππίας] Another famous sophist and rhetorician, a native of Elis. He was employed on diplomatic missions to various states, and, in particular, to Sparta (Hipp. Maj. 281 A, B). This mixture of the professor and politician was a characteristic common to the three sophists here mentioned (Ibid. 282 B, C). Hippias' specialty in science was astronomy (Hipp Maj 285 C ad in., Hipp. Min. 367 E ad fin   Cp Prot 315 C   He was also in the habit of lecturing on grammar and music (Hipp Maj. 285 D ad in ; Hipp. Min 368 D. Hippias' memory was extraordinarily retentive. Plato makes him boast that he could remember fifty names on once hearing them (Hipp Maj 285 E. Cp Philost, Lives of the Sophists, p. 210 ad in.   He would seem to have invented some artificial system of mnemonics (Hipp Min 368 D, Xen Conv IV. § 62). Hippias was considerably younger than Gorgias (Hipp Maj 282 E). He is treated with less respect by Plato than either Gorgias or Prodicus. We are allowed to see that the main feature of his character was an overweening vanity. Yet he appears to have had a good deal to be vain of, and to have been, in fact, a sort of 'admirable Crichton' of his day. We are told that he appeared on one occasion at Olympia with every article of his apparel and equipment—his ring, seal, flesh-scraper, oil-flask, shoes, cloak, tunic—made by his own hands. To crown all, he wore a girdle resembling the most costly Persian work which he had woven himself. Besides this he carried with him his own works in prose and poetry—epic, tragic, and dithyrambic (Hipp. Min. 368 B-D). Among the prose works of Hippias we have mention of one called the Trojan Dialogue, evidently an ἐπίδειξις, like that of Prodicus The scheme appears to have been simple—Nestor after the taking of Troy giving advice to Neoptolemus how to show himself a good man (Philost, Lives of the Sophists, p. 210).

ἰὼν εἰς ἑκάστην κτλ] One of the chief causes which lent invidiousness to the pretensions of the Sophists was this claim, that they, coming as strangers to a city, were better qualified to educate the young men than their own relations. See Prot 316 C, D; Hipp. Maj. 283 E.

πείθουσι] The subject τούτων ἕκαστος is virtually plural, so that there is nothing very startling in this change of number   Plato is everywhere colloquial, but nowhere more so than in the Apology, where it is part of his dramatic purpose to contrast the simple speech of Socrates with the laboured oratory of the law-courts. If the words in brackets, οἷός τ' ἐστίν, were retained, we would have a violent anacoluthon, or change of construction. There is nothing corresponding to them in the Theages (127 E, 128 A), in which the whole of this passage is reproduced.

20 A ἐπεί] See note above on 19 E

ἐπιδημοῦντα] Notice that verbs of seeing, knowing, &c, are constructed with a participle.

Καλλίᾳ τῷ Ἱππονίκου] Surnamed 'the wealthy.' His house was the largest and richest in Athens See Prot. 337 D, in which dialogue not only Protagoras himself is represented as being entertained by Callias, but also Prodicus of Ceos, Hippias of Elis, and many others of less note (314 B, C. Cp Xen Conv. I § 5) He had another house at the Peiraeus, which is the scene of Xenophon's Symposium. His mother married Pericles as her second husband, to whom she was already related by blood, and had by him two sons, Paralus and Xanthippus (Prot 314 E, 315 A; Meno 94 B; Plut. Pericles 16 5) His brother Hermogenes is one of the interlocutors in the Cratylus (384 A ad fin, 391 B) Callias seems especially to have imbibed the teaching of Protagoras (Crat 391 C; Theaet 165 A ad in.). His passion for philosophy is referred to in many passages of Plato, e g Prot 335 D. Ὦ παῖ Ἱππονίκου, ἀεὶ μὲν ἔγωγέ σου τὴν φιλοσοφίαν ἄγαμαι but it does not seem to have produced any beneficial effect upon his character, as he is said to have been a spendthrift and a profligate His reputation, however, has suffered at the hands of his enemy Andocides

ἀνηρόμην] In Attic prose ἠρόμην is commonly used as the aorist of ἐρωτάω See, for instance, Prot 350 C, εἰ δὲ καὶ οἱ θαρραλέοι ἀνδρεῖοι, οὐκ ἠρωτήθην εἰ γάρ με τότε ἤρου κ τ.λ

δύο υἱεῖς] See Andocides de Mysteriis, §§ 126, 7

ἀρετήν] Notice that adjectives can be followed by a cognate B accusative as well as verbs Cp below D, ταύτην εἶναι σοφός. 22 C, D; Meno 93 B

τῆς ἀνθρωπίνης τε καὶ πολιτικῆς] 'The virtue which makes a man and a citizen' This was exactly what the Sophists claimed to impart. See Prot. 318 E

ἐπιστήμων] To Plato's mind there was an etymological connection between ἐπιστήμων and ἐπιστάτης

κτῆσιν] 'Owing to your having sons.' κτάομαι in the present means 'to acquire,' κέκτημαι in the perfect 'to possess' The verbal substantive κτῆσις has sometimes the one meaning and sometimes the other In Euthyd. 228 D, for instance, it distinctly means 'acquisition,' Ἡ δέ γε φιλοσοφία κτῆσις ἐπιστήμης So also Gorg 478 C For the other meaning 'possession,' which it has here, cp. Rep I 331 B; Arist. Eth. Nic. I (8) § 9, IV. (1) §§ 7, 23.

Τίς, ἦν δ' ἐγώ κ τ λ.] The rapid succession of questions is meant to indicate the eagerness of the speaker. They are answered with a succinctness which might satisfy the most impatient. Πάριος is in reply to ποδαπός.

Εὐηνός] Evenus is referred to as a poet in Phaedo 60 D; certain technicalities of rhetoric are ascribed to him in Phaedrus 267 A

ἐμμελῶς] 'Teaches so cheaply' From meaning 'harmonious,' or 'well-proportioned,' ἐμμελής came to mean 'small.' Cp. Laws 760 A, τρεῖς εἰς τὰ μέγιστα ἱερά, δύο δ' εἰς τὰ σμικρότερα, πρὸς δὲ τὰ ἐμμελέστατα ἕνα; Arist. Pol. VII. 6. § 8, κεκτημένοι τῷ μεγέθει πόλιν ἐτέρων ἐμμελεστέραν. The change in the meaning of ἐμμελής somewhat resembles that of the Latin *gracilis*, which in prose commonly means 'thin.' Cp also ἄξιος and the German *billig*.

ἐκαλλυνόμην τε καὶ ἡβρυνόμην ἄν] 'Would have prided and plumed myself'

ἀλλ' οὐ γάρ] 'But indeed I don't know them.' The ellipse theory would here require us to fill up thus · ἀλλ' (οὐ καλλύνομαι τε καὶ ἁβρύνομαι), οὐ γὰρ ἐπίσταμαι. See note on 19 C, ἀλλὰ γάρ

τὸ σὸν τί ἐστι πρᾶγμα,] 'How stands the case with you?' Crito 53 D.

[εἰ μή τι ἔπραττες κ τ λ.] These words simply repeat the clause above, σοῦ γε οὐδέν κ.τ.λ They may nevertheless be genuine, as an emphatic tautology is common enough in Plato. Riddell registers it, under the title of 'Binary Structure,' as one of the prominent features of his style. Digest, § 204

εὖ μέντοι ἴστε] For μέντοι balancing μέν, in place of the usual δέ, cp. 38 D μέντοι really goes with ἐρῶ, εὖ ἴστε being adverbial.

ἔσχηκα] See note on 19 A, ἐξελέσθαι. . χρόνῳ

ποίαν δὴ σοφίαν ταύτην;] The words are drawn into the accusative through the influence of the διά preceding. Translate 'Of what kind then is this wisdom through which I have obtained it?' Cp Gorg. 449 D, E, περὶ λόγους Ποίους τούτους; The same attraction may take place where there is no preposition preceding, as in Gorg. 462 E, Τίνος λέγεις ταύτης. Here the word preceding is in the genitive.

ἥπερ] Supply τοιαύτη ἐστίν

ταύτην εἶναι σοφός] Cp. the words which follow, μείζω τινά κ τ λ., and see note on 20 B, τὴν προσήκουσαν ἀρετήν

φησί] 'Says I do' φημί is 'I assert,' οὐ φημί, 'I deny'

μὴ θορυβήσητε] The aorist subjunctive forbids a particular act in Greek, like the perfect subjunctive in Latin.

μέγα λέγειν] 'To be saying something big.' Cp. Arist. Eth. Nic I. (4). § 3. συνειδότες δ' ἑαυτοῖς ἄγνοιαν τοὺς μέγα τι καὶ ὑπὲρ αὑτοὺς λέγοντας θαυμάζουσιν The μεγαληγορία of Socrates was noticed by all who gave an account of his defence. See Xenophon, Apol. Soc. § 1. Cicero, De Oratore, ch. 54, says of him, 'Ita in iudicio capitis pro se ipse dixit, ut non supplex aut reus, sed magister aut dominus videretur esse iudicum.'

οὐ γὰρ ἐμὸν ἐρῶ τὸν λόγον] The rule of Greek syntax that the subject has the article and the predicate not, extends to the case of a secondary and tertiary predicate. We have here two statements in a compressed form:

(1) ἐρῶ λόγον
(2) ὁ λόγος οὐκ ἐμὸς ἔσται.

The same principle applies to the next clause also.

ἀλλ' εἰς ἀξιόχρεων κ τ λ.] 'But I shall refer it (τὸν λόγον) to a speaker whom you may trust' It is difficult to say whether ὑμῖν should be taken immediately with ἀξιόχρεων or with the sentence generally as a *dativus commodi* after ἀνοίσω.

Χαιρεφῶντα] Chaerephon, of the Sphettian deme, was one of the most devoted adherents of Socrates. He associated with him for the sake of mental and moral improvement, and is mentioned by Xenophon as one who had brought no discredit on the teachings of his master (Mem I 2. § 48). His disposition was impulsive and excitable (Charm 153 B). Chaerephon had a younger brother, Chaerecrates Memorabilia II. 2 contains an exhortation to Chaerecrates to conciliate Chaerephon, with whom he was at variance. Chaerephon figures in the Charmides and in the Gorgias, where we are told that he was a friend of that eminent teacher (Gorg 447 B) In personal appearance Chaerephon was sickly, lean and darkcomplexioned. This explains some of the uncomplimentary allusions of the Comic poets, who were peculiarly bitter in their attacks upon him, partly perhaps for political reasons, as he was evidently a warm partisan. Aristophanes in the Birds calls him an owl (line 1296). In the Wasps he compares him to a sallow woman (line 1413); in the lost play of the Seasons he nicknamed him 'the son of night.' To the same effect is the epithet πύξινος bestowed upon him by Eupolis in the Cities. His poverty, or, it may be, his asceticism, is jeered at in the Clouds, 103, 4—

τοὺς ὠχριῶντας, τοὺς ἀνυποδήτους λέγεις·
ὦν ὁ κακοδαίμων Σωκράτης καὶ Χαιρεφῶν

Similarly Cratinus called him αὐχμηρὸν καὶ πένητα. Even the moral character of Chaerephon did not escape scatheless. Aristophanes called him a sycophant in one play and a thief in another, while Eupolis accused him of toadying Callias. On the whole, then, Chaerephon was pretty well known to the Athenians See the Scholiast on this passage. For other allusions to him in the Clouds see lines 144, 156, 504, 832, 1465. Chaerephon, we see, was already dead when Socrates was brought to trial. Philostratus (p 203) says that his health was affected by study.

τὴν φυγὴν ταύτην] 'The recent exile,' referring to the expulsion 21 A of the popular party from Athens in the time of the Thirty Tyrants, whose usurpation lasted from June 404 B C. to February 403. The restoration of the democracy was effected in the following year (B C. 403-402), memorable in Athenian history under the title of the archonship of Eucleides.

ὡς σφοδρός] ἦν has to be supplied from the preceding clause. 'How energetic in whatever he set to work at!' Cp. Charm. 153 B, ἅτε καὶ μανικὸς ὤν.

ὅπερ λέγω] 'As I say' Cp. 24 A ad in, 27 B ad in, 29 D ad in The request above. μὴ θορυβήσητε, is repeated now in a more general form.

ἀνεῖλεν] The words of the oracle are recorded by the Scholiast—

σοφὸς Σοφοκλῆς, σοφώτερος Εὐριπίδης·
ἀνδρῶν δ' ἁπάντων Σωκράτης σοφώτατος.

The second line only is quoted by Diogenes. Perhaps a δέ has dropped out before the Εὐριπίδης in the first

ὁ ἀδελφός] Doubtless the Chaerecrates already referred to See note on 20 E, Χαιρεφῶντα.

οὐ γὰρ θέμις αὐτῷ] We see here that growing moral conception of the divine nature, which led to the revolt of the philosophers against mythology.

αὐτοῦ] 'Into it,' i.e. into the matter. This vague use of the pronoun is not uncommon. See Meno 73 C, τί αὐτό φησι.

μαντεῖον] This word here evidently means 'the divine utterance,' not the place of divination, which is a meaning it often bears.

τῷ χρησμῷ] 'The oracle.' χρησμός is properly the answer given by an oracle, like μαντεῖον just above, but it is here personified out of reverence, to avoid the appearance of calling the god to account.

ὅτι] Notice that ὅτι is used with the direct as well as with the oblique narration, unlike 'that' in English, which is confined to the latter.

ἔφησθα] For the form cp ἦσθα, ᾔεισθα, οἶσθα.

ὀνόματι γάρ] γάρ explains why the mere pronoun τοῦτον is used instead of the proper name 'I say him, for,' etc.

πρὸς ὃν ἐγὼ σκοπῶν κ τ.λ] 'In whose case I had on inquiry some such experience as this' For the construction πάσχειν πρός τινα cp. Gorg. 485 B, καὶ ἔγωγε ὁμοιότατον πάσχω πρὸς τοὺς φιλοσοφοῦντας ὥσπερ πρὸς τοὺς ψελλιζομένους καὶ παίζοντας.

καὶ διαλεγόμενος αὐτῷ] This is coordinate with διασκοπῶν at the beginning of the sentence

ἔδοξέ μοι] Here we have a violent anacoluthon, or, to put it frankly, a piece of bad grammar After the participle διαλεγόμενος we should have expected some such construction as the ἐλογιζόμην ὅτι, which follows in D. Instead of which the participle is left to look after itself, thus forming a *nominativus pendens*, and the sentence is finished in the impersonal form. For similar instances of changed construction see Riddell, Digest of Idioms, § 271.

ἀπηχθόμην] 'Got myself disliked.' Cp Philebus 58 C, οὐδὲ γὰρ D ἀπεχθήσει Γοργίᾳ. This is an instance of what Riddell calls the semi-middle sense of the verb See Digest, § 88. Cp. note on 35 C, ἐθίζεσθαι.

κινδυνεύει] On the force of κινδυνεύω see L and S. sub voce, 4 b.

καλὸν κἀγαθόν] This expression is generally used in the masculine, and implies the *ne plus ultra* of perfection, the man who is beautiful both without and within—the finished result of γυμναστική and μουσική. For the neuter use cp Arist Eth. Nic. I. (8.) § 9, τῶν ἐν τῷ βίῳ καλῶν κἀγαθῶν.

αἰσθανόμενος μέν κ.τ.λ.] 'Perceiving indeed with pain and apprehension.' E

ἰτέον οὖν] This may be dependent on ἐδόκει with εἶναι understood; but it is more likely that we have here a sudden transition to the direct narration, 'So I must go,' etc.

τὸν χρησμόν, τί λέγει] 'The meaning of the oracle.' The Greek idiom is well known by which the subject of the succeeding verb becomes the object of the preceding one. The sentence as we have it is much livelier than if the strict syntax were followed—σκοποῦντι ὅ,τι λέγοι ὁ χρησμός.

νὴ τὸν κύνα] The Scholiast quotes Cratinus in the Cheirons—
οἷς ἦν μέγιστος ὅρκος ἅπαντι λόγῳ κύων,
ἔπειτα χῆν· θεοὺς δ' ἐσίγων—
and tells us that such oaths as those by the dog, the goose, the plane-tree (see Phaedrus 236 E ad in.), the ram, and so on, were resorted to for the avoidance of profanity. For the oath by the goose, see Aristophanes, Birds 521—
Λάμπων δ' ὄμνυσ' ἔτι καὶ νυνὶ τὸν χῆν', ὅταν ἐξαπατᾷ τι.
It is probably only Plato's fun to identify 'the dog' with the Egyptian god Anubis (Gorg. 482 B, μὰ τὸν κύνα τὸν Αἰγυπτίων θεόν). It has been suggested that νὴ τὸν χῆνα is a disguise for νὴ τὸν Ζῆνα, like *potz-tausend*, *morbleu* and many other modern oaths.

ὀλίγου δεῖν κ.τ.λ.] 'To be nearly (lit within a little of being) 22 A the most deficient.' The τοῦ belongs to εἶναι. The phrase is usually followed by a simple infinitive, whether it is used personally, as in 30 D, 37 B, or impersonally, as in 35 D.

κατὰ τὸν θεόν] Socrates regards the statement of the god as implying a command to prove its truth.

APOLOGY, NOTES. 22 A, B.

ὥσπερ πόνους τινὰς πονοῦντος] He compares his task of convincing mankind of their ignorance to the labours of a Hercules. πονοῦντος agrees with the ἐμοῦ implied in ἐμήν.

ἵνα μοι κ τ λ.] 'In order that I might have the divine declaration set quite above dispute' Socrates, though puzzled by the oracle, is anxious to vindicate the truth of the deity. Riddell distinguishes between μαντεῖον and μαντεία, taking the former to signify the expression and the latter the meaning, so that μαντεία stands to μαντεῖον in the same relation as the judgment to the proposition in logic. The propositions of an oracle, as is well known, were peculiarly liable to equivocation and amphiboly, so that the μαντεῖον might differ seriously from the μαντεία, as in the historical instances of Croesus and Pyrrhus. In its primary meaning μαντεία signifies the process of divination, not, as here, the product. Hermann emends the text by the conjecture κἂν ἐλεγκτός, which represents it as the object of Socrates to refute the oracle. This does not seem consistent with the words above in 21 B, οὐ γὰρ δήπου ψεύδεταί γε· οὐ γὰρ θέμις αὐτῷ, while on the other hand it fits in better with the words which follow, ὡς ἐνταῦθα ἐπ' αὐτοφώρῳ καταληψόμενος ἐμαυτὸν ἀμαθέστερον ἐκείνων ὄντα. In either case there is a slight difficulty, but complete consistency cannot be looked for in a dilemma between piety and politeness

τούς τε τῶν τραγῳδιῶν κ τ.λ] Cp. Hipp Min 368 C, πρὸς δὲ τούτοις ποιήματα ἔχων ἐλθεῖν, καὶ ἔπη καὶ τραγῳδίας καὶ διθυράμβους, also Xen Mem I 4 § 3, ἐπὶ μὲν τοίνυν ἐπῶν ποιήσει Ὅμηρον ἔγωγε μάλιστα τεθαύμακα, ἐπὶ δὲ διθυράμβῳ Μελανιππίδην, ἐπὶ δὲ τραγῳδίᾳ Σοφοκλέα.

B διθυράμβων] When Plato is speaking technically, he confines διθύραμβος to a song relating to the birth of Bacchus, coordinating it with ὕμνοι, θρῆνοι, παιῶνες and νόμοι as various species of ᾠδαί, Laws 700 B.

καὶ τοὺς ἄλλους] For a fuller list of species of poetry see Ion 534 C, ὁ μὲν (οἷός τε ποιεῖν καλῶς) διθυράμβους, ὁ δὲ ἐγκώμια, ὁ δὲ ὑπορχήματα, ὁ δ' ἔπη, ὁ δ' ἰάμβους

ἐπ' αὐτοφώρῳ] 'Palpably' Properly said of a thief (φώρ, *fur*) caught in the very act (αὐτο-).

αὐτοῖς] Dative of the agent. πεπραγματεῦσθαι is passive.

οἱ παρόντες] 'Who were present.' The participle is in the imperfect tense

ἔγνων] See note on 25 D, ἔγνωκας.

ἐν ὀλίγῳ] 'In short.' The meaning is the same as that of ἐνὶ λόγῳ, which Hermann conjectured in place of it. Riddell compares Symp 217 A, ἐν βραχεῖ.

φύσει τινὶ καὶ ἐνθουσιάζοντες] 'Owing to a sort of instinct and C divine afflatus.' This theory of poetry as a form of inspiration meets us everywhere in Plato, e.g. Phaedrus 245 A; Meno 99 D, Ion 533 D—534 E.

The participle ἐνθουσιάζοντες is here equivalent to a dative of manner.

πάθος .. πεπονθότες] Accusative of the internal object. πάθος πεπονθέναι means 'to be in a certain state.' Cp. ὅ τι .. πεπόνθατε, 17 A.

ᾐσθόμην αὐτῶν .. οἰομένων] The genitive after a verb of perception, and the participle, instead of infinitive, as after verbs of seeing, knowing, etc. Cp 20 A, ἐπιδημοῦντα.

σοφωτάτων εἶναι] After οἰομένων, the case being preserved

καὶ ἐντεῦθεν] 'From them too' Like *inde* and *unde* in Latin, ἐντεῦθεν is sometimes used of persons

τῷ αὐτῷ] Cp 21 D, σμικρῷ τινι κ.τ.λ.

τούτους κ.τ.λ.] See note on 21 E, τὸν χρησμόν, τί λέγει. D

εὑρήσοιμι] Future optative, which is found in oblique oration only. The direct statement would be οἶδα ὅτι εὑρήσω.

ἔχειν ἁμάρτημα] 'To be under a mistake,' 'make a mistake.' With ποιηταί supply εἶχον.

ἠξίου] 'Claimed'

ἀπέκρυπτεν] 'Threw into the shade.' The assumption of universal knowledge was a mistake which outweighed in importance the value of their specific skill in handicraft

πότερα δεξαίμην ἄν] 'Whether I would choose.' Literally E 'would accept' (if the choice were offered).

οὕτως ὥσπερ ἐγὼ ἔχειν] 'To be as I am' This is the meaning of ἔχω with adverbs—ἔχειν καλῶς, κακῶς, etc But below ἔχειν ἃ ἐκεῖνοι ἔχουσιν means ' to have what they have,' their knowledge and their ignorance.

οἷαι χαλεπώταται] 'Of a kind that are the bitterest.' Supply 23 A εἰσί

ὄνομα δὲ τοῦτο κ.τ.λ.] 'And I am called by this name, that I am wise.' Riddell. Lit. 'I am called by name, this, &c.' We might have expected τὸ εἶναί με σοφόν The nominative is due to the fact that Socrates is himself the subject. For a similar construction with the addition of the article cp. Symp. 173 D, ταύτην τὴν ἐπωνυμίαν ἔλαβες τὸ μανικὸς καλεῖσθαι.

οἱ παρόντες] 'The bystanders'

ἃ ἂν ἄλλον ἐξελέγξω] 'Wherein I have refuted another.' Ἐξελέγχω can take two accusatives: (1) of the person; (2) of the thing.

τὸ δὲ κινδυνεύει] Perhaps it is best, with Riddell in his Digest, § 19 (though not in his text), to separate τὸ δέ by a comma from κινδυνεύει. τὸ δέ introduces a counter-statement, and may be rendered 'whereas,' 'but in fact,' or quite literally, 'but for that matter.' For a similar use of τὸ δέ cp. Meno 97 C, τὸ δὲ ἄρα καὶ δόξα ἦν ἀληθής, 'whereas after all there was also right opinion.' Other instances are Theaet. 157 B, 183 A, 207 B; Soph. 244 A; Symp 198 D; Prot. 344 E; Rep 340 D, 443 C; Laws 803 D.

ὁ θεός] This was probably intended to be understood of Apollo, and yet did not quite mean so in Plato's mind

καὶ οὐδενός] An instance of the alternative use of καί 'Little or nothing'

οὐ λέγει τὸν Σωκράτη] 'Not to mean the individual, Socrates'

ἔγνωκεν] See note on 25 D, ἔγνωκας

ἄν τινα οἴωμαι] 'Anyone whom I may imagine' Supply τοῦτον before ζητῶ καὶ ἐρευνῶ. ἄν is contracted from ἐάν. The verbs of seeking, ζητῶ καὶ ἐρευνῶ, take a double accusative, one of the person and another of the thing, ταῦτα. ταῦτα = διὰ ταῦτα, as Mr. Adam takes it. Cp. Xen. Anab IV. 1. § 21 ταῦτ' ἐγὼ ἔσπευδον καὶ διὰ τοῦτό σε οὐχ ὑπέμενον.

ἐν πενίᾳ μυρίᾳ] 'In untold poverty' μυρίος denotes anything that is beyond counting; μύριος means definitely ten thousand. The use of μυρίος for πολύς is found several times in Plato Aristotle mentions it as a use of the specific for the general word, and so more suitable to poetry than prose. In English we use 'thousand' and 'thousands' to express an indefinitely large number; sometimes 'millions.' The Romans did not get beyond six hundred, *sexcenti*.

On the poverty of Socrates cp 31 C, 36 D, 38 B. In the last of these passages Socrates says that he thinks he could pay a fine of a mina (about £4). By Xenophon his whole property is estimated at 5 minae (Oecon. II. § 3). It is recorded of Socrates that when he looked at the variety of goods for sale, he said to himself, 'How many things there are which I have no need of!' (Diog. Laert II. § 25). See also Rep 337 D; Xen. Mem. I. 2. § 1. Oecon. XI. 3.

οἷς μάλιστα σχολή ἐστιν] To attend the lectures and discourses of the Sophists, among whom Socrates, despite his idiosyncrasies, must be reckoned, was the Greek equivalent to a university education among ourselves.

οἱ τῶν πλουσιωτάτων] 'The sons of the wealthiest citizens' Supply υἱεῖς from the νέοι preceding, or repeat νέοι itself, like Juvenal's—

'pinnirapi cultos iuvenes iuvenesque lanistae' (III. 158).

αὐτόματοι] With ἐπακολουθοῦντες. He means that these young men had not been formally committed to his charge by their parents, and that he was under no tutorial relations to them. Cp. Xen. Mem I. 2. § 18

ἀκούοντες ἐξεταζομένων] See note on 22 C, ᾐσθόμην κ.τ λ.

εἶτ' ἐπιχειροῦσιν] 'And so try.' In the Republic, 539 B, Plato compares the delight of the young in argument to that of puppies in worrying the first thing they meet He would reserve dialectic for men of mature years

ἐντεῦθεν] 'As a consequence.' The odium reverted upon Socrates, as he was the originator of this unpleasant system of examination

Σωκράτης τίς ἐστι] τίς is predicate 'Socrates is a most pestilent fellow.' Contrast with this the construction in 18 B, ὡς ἔστι τις Σωκράτης, where τις goes with Σωκράτης and ἔστι is the substantive verb.

πρόχειρα] A metaphor from a stone or other missile which is **D** ready to hand against some one We have an excellent illustration of the kind of thing referred to in the Symposium of Xenophon, in which the showman, irritated with Socrates for engrossing the attention of the guests by his conversation, calls him μετέωρον φροντιστής, and asks him how many flea's paces he is off from him Xen. Conv. VI. §§ 6-8).

ὅτι τὰ μετέωρα] Supply διαφθείρει τοὺς νέους διδάσκων from above. The accusatives τὰ μετέωρα καὶ τὰ ὑπὸ γῆς and also the infinitives νομίζειν and ποιεῖν, which are coordinate with them, are governed by διδάσκων understood.

ἅτε . . ὄντες] 'Seeing that they are.' Lit 'as being.' ἅτε is much the same in sense as ὡς, but is more exclusively used to give a reason.

ξυντεταγμένως] 'In set array.' Riddell Perhaps Mr Adam is right in understanding it as = Latin composite, 'in studied language.' There is another reading, ξυντεταμένως, which would mean 'earnestly.'

ἐκ τούτων] 'It is on this ground.' **E**

Μέλητος] See note on 19 B.

Ἄνυτος] Anytus was a prominent leader of the popular party at Athens (Xen Hell II 3 § 42). His father, Anthemion, had made his fortune as a tanner (see Meno 90 A, and Scholiast on Apology). Hence the propriety of his appearing in a double capacity as champion ὑπὲρ τῶν δημιουργῶν καὶ τῶν πολιτικῶν

Λύκων δὲ ὑπὲρ τῶν ῥητόρων] The Scholiast informs us that **24 A** Lycon was an Ionian by extraction, and belonged to the deme of

Thoricus   He is called a 'demagogue' by Diogenes Laertius, II §
38 ad fin.   His poverty excited the ridicule of the comic poets
Cratinus and Aristophanes   The more serious charge of treason is
brought against him in the Hostage ("Ομηρος" of Metagenes, one of
the *aiti quorum comoedia prisca virorum est*.—

...... καὶ Λύκων ἐνταῦθά που
... προδοὺς Ναύπακτον ἀργύριον λαβὼν
ἀγορᾶς ἄγαλμα ξενικὸν ἐμπορεύεται

We are told that Eupolis in the Friends satirized his wife
Rhodia   The Scholiast identifies the accuser of Socrates with Lycon,
the father of Autolycus, the youth in whose honour the Symposium
of Xenophon is represented as having been given, and adds that
Lycon was satirized as a stranger in the play of Eupolis called
'The First Autolycus'   This play is assigned to B C. 420.   The
identification of the two persons appears highly improbable on
chronological and other grounds   There is a Lycon mentioned in
an uncomplimentary context by Aristophanes, Wasps 1301.

οὔτε μέγα οὔτε σμικρόν]   The frequent recurrence of this phrase
in the Apology is perhaps intentional   Cp. 19 C, D, 21 B; 26 B
It may have been a trick of speaking on the part of Socrates,
which Plato has been careful to reproduce

οὐδ' ὑποστειλάμενος]   Ὑποστέλλω is used of lowering or furling
a sail   The metaphors of a nation give us a clue to their habitual
pursuits   Those of the Athenians are mostly naval, legal, or
gymnastic.

τοῖς αὐτοῖς]   'Through the same things'

καὶ ὅτι αὕτη κ τ. λ]   'And that this is the meaning of the prejudice against me, and these the causes of it '

B   αὕτη ἔστω κ.τ.λ.]   'Let this be a sufficient defence before
you '   Αὕτη is attracted into the gender of the predicate ἀπολογία, being put for τοῦτο.   This is the prevailing construction in
Greek.

πρὸς δὲ Μέλητον]   Euripides is instinct with the spirit of the
law-courts.   It is worth while to compare his Hecuba, lines 1195, 6—
καί μοι τὸ μὲν σὸν ὧδε φροιμίοις ἔχει
πρὸς τόνδε δ' εἶμι, καὶ λόγοις ἀμείψομαι.

λάβωμεν αὖ]   αὖ does no more than repeat the αὖθις at the
beginning of the sentence.

ἀντωμοσίαν]   See note on 19 B

Σωκράτη φησὶν ἀδικεῖν κ.τ.λ]   Xenophon, Mem I. 1. § 1, gives
us the indictment in the direct narration, without vouching for its
literal accuracy, as he introduces it by τοιάδε τις ἦν.   'Αδικεῖ
Σωκράτης οὓς μὲν ἡ πόλις νομίζει θεοὺς οὐ νομίζων, ἕτερα δὲ καινὰ

APOLOGY, NOTES. 24 B–25 A.

δαιμόνια εἰσφέρων· ἀδικεῖ δὲ καὶ τοὺς νέους διαφθείρων. In the Apologia Socratis § 10, where it is repeated in the oblique narration, the wording is substantially the same—κατηγόρησαν αὐτοῦ οἱ ἀντίδικοι ὡς οὓς μὲν ἡ πόλις νομίζει θεοὺς οὐ νομίζοι, ἕτερα δὲ καινὰ δαιμόνια εἰσφέροι καὶ τοὺς νέους διαφθείροι. Diogenes Laertius II. § 40 states on the authority of Favorinus, a writer of the age of Hadrian, that the indictment was preserved in the Metroum. He quotes it in exactly the same form in which it is given by Xenophon, except that εἰσηγούμενος is used instead of εἰσφέρων. The indictment is followed by the words τίμημα θάνατος.

σπουδῇ χαριεντίζεται] An instance of oxymoron, or intentional paradox. For illustrations of this figure of speech see Farrar's Greek Syntax, § 315 C. Riddell renders it 'is playing off a jest under solemn forms.'

καί μοι δεῦρο κ.τ.λ.] The imaginary heckling of Meletus which follows is in due form of law, being the ἐρώτησις, to which either party was bound to submit at the instance of the other. See 25 D, ἀπόκριναι, ὦ 'γαθέ· καὶ γὰρ ὁ νόμος κελεύει ἀποκρίνεσθαι: also 27 C. In Demosthenes, p. 1131 ad fin. (Κατὰ Στεφάνου Β, 10', a law is quoted to the following effect: τοῖν ἀντιδίκοιν ἐπάναγκες εἶναι ἀποκρίνασθαι ἀλλήλοις τὸ ἐρωτώμενον, μαρτυρεῖν δὲ μή. See Riddell, Introd p. xviii.

ἄλλο τι ἤ] A common interrogative formula in Plato, equivalent to the Latin *nonne*. To ask, 'Do you do anything else than such and such a thing?' is a roundabout way of indicating our belief that the person does the thing in question. On the same principle we insert a 'not' in English, when we wish to suggest an affirmative answer. 'Do you not consider it of great importance, etc.?'

ἐμὲ εἰσάγεις] ἐμέ appears to be under a double construction, being predicate to τὸν διαφθείροντα, while at the same time it is the direct object after εἰσάγεις. 'For having discovered their corrupter, as you assert, in me, you are bringing me up before them and accusing me.'

πολλὴν ἀφθονίαν] The number of judges was at least 500.

μὴ οἱ ἐν τῇ ἐκκλησίᾳ] Let it be borne in mind that while οὐ expects the answer Yes, μή expects the answer No.

καλοὺς κἀγαθούς] See note on 21 D.

Πολλήν γ' ἐμοῦ κατέγνωκας δυστυχίαν] Translate, 'I am very unfortunate in your opinion.' Καταγιγνώσκειν τινός means to form an estimate of somebody. It may be used of favourable or unfavourable judgments indifferently. Cp Meno 76 C, καὶ ἅμα ἐμοῦ ἴσως κατέγνωκας, ὅτι εἰμὶ ἥττων τῶν καλῶν: Xen. Oec. II. § 1, ἦ κατέγνωκας ἡμῶν, ὦ Σώκρατες, ἱκανῶς πλουτεῖν;

23

B πάντες ἄνθρωποι εἶναι] Supply δοκοῦσι from the impersonal δοκεῖ preceding. Cp Meno 72 D, ἄλλη μὲν ἀνδρὸς εἶναι

τοὐναντίον τούτου πᾶν] These words should perhaps be considered subject to δοκεῖ understood, and explained by the εἷς μέν τις which follows in apposition. For a different view see Riddell, Dig § 13.

οὐ φῆτε] How entirely the οὐ coalesces with φημί is plain from the fact that in any other case we should here require μή. Cp. note on φησί, 20 E.

C ἀμέλειαν] Socrates has throughout been playing on the name Meletus. Cp § 24 C, D; 26 B. For other instances of puns in Plato see Riddell, Digest § 323.

ὦ πρὸς Διός, Μέλητε] It looks as though the ὦ really belonged to the vocative Μέλητε, and were separated only through that confusion of expression which is so common a feature in adjurations. Similarly in Meno 71 D, ὦ πρὸς θεῶν, Μένων, τί φῆς ἀρετὴν εἶναι; But this idea has to be abandoned when we find the same expression occurring where there is no vocative at all, as below 26 E, ἀλλ' ὦ πρὸς Διός, οὑτωσί σοι δοκῶ κ.τ.λ. Cp Rep 332 C, Ὦ πρὸς Διός, ἦν δ' ἐγώ, εἰ οὖν τις αὐτὸν ἤρετο

ἐν πολίταις χρηστοῖς ἢ πονηροῖς] The position of the adjectives throws a predicative force upon them. Translate, 'Is it better to have the fellow-citizens among whom one dwells good or bad?'

ὦ 'τᾶν] Nothing is really known as to the origin and meaning of this mysterious form of address, except that it is a formula of politeness. It is plural as well as singular. See Liddell and Scott, under ἔτης and τᾶν.

D καὶ γὰρ ὁ νόμος κελεύει ἀποκρίνεσθαι] See note on καί μοι δεῦρο κ.τ.λ., 24 C.

τηλικούτου ὄντος τηλικόσδε ὤν] 'Are you at your age so much wiser than I at mine?' The usual meaning of the pronouns (see note on τῇδε τῇ ἡλικίᾳ, 17 C) is here exactly reversed. For τηλικόσδε used by the speaker of himself see below 34 E, 37 D; Crito 49 A ad fin.; Theaet. 177 C. and for τηλικοῦτος used of another see Prot. 361 E; Gorg. 466 A, 489 B ad fin. In Crito 43 B we have τηλικοῦτος used both in the first and second person, or rather, without distinction of person.

ἔγνωκας] The aorist ἔγνων in 22 B ad fin expresses an act; the perfect here expresses the state which is the result of that act. ἔγνων is 'I recognised,' ἔγνωκας is 'you are in the state of having recognised,' and so, 'you know.' Further on, 27 A, the future γνώσεται may be rendered 'find out,' and so with the aorist in 33 D ad in.

ὑπ' αὐτοῦ] 'At his hands' κακόν τι λαβεῖν is virtually passive. **E**
οὐδένα] Supply πείθεσθαι   **26 A**
τοιούτων καὶ ἀκουσίων] If the words in brackets are genuine, the καί is explanatory of τοιούτων. It may be omitted in translating
ἐὰν μάθω] 'If I am instructed.' Μανθάνω is practically the passive of διδάσκω, as πάσχω of ποιέω, θνήσκω of κτείνω, κεῖμαι of τίθημι, ὀφλισκάνω of καταδικάζω, φεύγω of διώκω, εἰσιέναι of εἰσάγειν.
ἢ δῆλον δὴ ὅτι] Supply φῄς με διαφθείρειν τοὺς νεωτέρους. **B**
ὧν] For the simple genitive after λόγος Stallbaum quotes Charm. 156 A, οὐ γάρ τι σοῦ ὀλίγος λόγος ἐστίν
τὸ παράπαν οὐ νομίζεις θεούς] This was the impression which **C** the bulk of his contemporaries entertained of Socrates. It is conveyed plainly enough in the Clouds, e.g. in the answer of Socrates to Strepsiades (247, 8)—

ποίους θεοὺς ὀμεῖ σύ; πρῶτον γὰρ θεοὶ
ἡμῖν νόμισμ' οὐκ ἔστι,

and in the epithet ὁ Μήλιος (line 831) which is bestowed upon him, with allusion of course to Diagoras, who was surnamed ἄθεος (Cic. De Nat Deor I. chs 1 and 23).

οὐδὲ ἥλιον οὐδὲ σελήνην] In the Symposium 220 D, Socrates is **D** recorded to have prayed to the Sun, ἔπειτα ᾤχετ' ἀπιὼν προσευξάμενος τῷ ἡλίῳ. The Sun and Moon were regarded as divine beings by the Ancients, quite apart from their personification as Apollo and Artemis Helios in the Odyssey appears as a distinct person from Apollo (Od VIII. cp. 271 with 323). Among the definitions of the sun given in the Ὅροι, which follow the Letters in Hermann's Plato, are these two—(1) ζῷον ἀΐδιον, (2) ἔμψυχον τὸ μέγιστον

Μὰ Δί'] Supply οὐ νομίζει. See note on 17 B.
τὸν μὲν ἥλιον κ.τ.λ] See Diog. Laert II. § 8, in his life of Anaxagoras, Οὗτος ἔλεγε τὸν ἥλιον μύδρον εἶναι διάπυρον, καὶ μείζω τῆς Πελοποννήσου.

τὴν δὲ σελήνην γῆν] 'And the moon earth' γῆν is probably meant to explain the substance of which the moon was made. But it would be consistent with the tenets of Anaxagoras to translate, 'and the moon an earth.' For Anaxagoras is recorded to have believed that rational animals were not confined to our world, and that the moon contained dwelling-places as well as hills and valleys (Ritter and Preller 57 a; Diog Laert. II. § 8).

'Ἀναξαγόρου] Anaxagoras of Clazomenae was born about B.C. 500. He was a man of wealth and position in his own country, but he resigned his patrimony to his kinsmen, and set out for Athens at the age of 20, just at the time of the Persian invasion,

B C. 480 Here he spent the next 30 years of his life in the study of natural philosophy. Among the most distinguished of his pupils were Pericles and Euripides and Archelaus, the instructor of Socrates. His guesses at truth appear in some instances to have been very successful. Thus he maintained that the moon derived its light from the sun (Crat 409 B). Also he taught the eternity and indestructibility of matter, and declared 'becoming' and 'perishing' to be merely other names for combination and separation (Ritter and Preller, § 49). But what renders his name of most importance in the history of philosophy was his declaration that intelligence (νοῦς) was the cause of all motion and order in the universe. He was indicted by the Athenians for impiety on account of his opinion about the sun. Hereupon he retired to Lampsacus, where he ended his days in honour at the age of 72. The accounts, however, of his trial and death are very conflicting. According to Hermippus of Smyrna (apud Diog. Laert II. § 13) he was pardoned by the Athenians on the personal intercession of Pericles, who declared himself to be his disciple, but committed suicide in disgust at the treatment to which he had been subjected. Anaxagoras was a man of lofty mind with a passionate zeal for penetrating the secrets of nature. When asked for what he had been born, he replied, 'To contemplate the sun and moon and heaven' The fragments that remain of his writings contain Ionic forms See his life in Diog Laert. II §§ 6–15, and the fragments in Ritter and Preller

οἴει αὐτοὺς ἀπείρους] The force of the οὕτω preceding is carried on to these words.

ὥστε οὐκ εἰδέναι] The rule is that ὥστε, when followed by the indicative, requires οὐ, when by the infinitive, μή. Thus, to use Shilleto's example, we should have, on the one hand, οὕτως ἄφρων ἦν ὥστε οὐκ ἐβούλετο and, on the other, οὕτως ἄφρων ἦν ὥστε μὴ βούλεσθαι The difference between these two forms of expression is that the indicative puts the fact prominently forward, while the infinitive rather regards the event as the natural outcome of its antecedent—more briefly, the indicative expresses the real, the infinitive the logical consequence. Now when the infinitive is necessitated by the change from the direct to the oblique narration, this distinction would be lost, were the οὐ changed into μή. Hence when stress is meant to be laid upon the matter of fact, the οὐ of direct narration is retained in the oblique Here the direct statement would have been οὕτως ἄπειροί εἰσιν, ὥστε οὐκ ἴσασι See Shilleto, Demosth De Fals Leg, Appendix B.

τὰ Ἀναξαγόρου βιβλία] His principal work was a treatise on

nature, which Diogenes Laertius (II. § 6) tells us was 'written in an agreeable and elevated style.'

καὶ δὴ καί] 'And, I suppose.'

εἰ πάνυ πολλοῦ] 'At the most.' Cp. Alcib 123 C, ἄξιος μνῶν E πεντήκοντα, εἰ πάνυ πολλοῦ. Similarly ἐὰν πάμπολυ, Gorg. 511 D. Riddell

δραχμῆς ἐκ τῆς ὀρχήστρας] Three views have been held as to the meaning of this passage—

(1) That the orchestra of the theatre of Dionysus was used for the sale of books, when performances were not going on, and that the works of Anaxagoras could occasionally be bought there for rather less than a drachma

(2) That in return for the drachma which a theatre-goer might be supposed to pay, at the most, for a three days' performance, he was liable to be treated to the doctrines of Anaxagoras, so much had they become part of the common mental stock of Athens. Euripides was specially infected with the new learning See for instance Orestes 983

(3) That ὀρχήστρα here means a part of the Agora used for public performances, and where books may be supposed to have been sold. In the Platonic glossary of Timaeus the Sophist a second meaning is given for ὀρχήστρα, thus—τύπος ἐπιφανὴς εἰς πανήγυριν, ἔνθα Ἁρμοδίου καὶ Ἀριστογείτονος εἰκόνες. From Aristoph. Eccles. 681, 2, it appears that the statue of Harmodius was in the Agora

This last view is perhaps the right one. That a work on philosophy could be bought for so low a price as a drachma (roughly = a franc) at Athens, is, as Mr. Adam points out, the less surprising when taken in conjunction with Plato's other statement (Gorg 511 D), that 2 drachmas would be a high price to pay for the transport of a man with all his goods and family from Pontus or Egypt to Athens.

Ἄπιστος . καὶ . . . σαυτῷ] Because, as Socrates is going to show, he was contradicting himself. 'You are undeserving of credit, Meletus, and that too indeed, as it seems to me, in your own eyes.'

ὥσπερ αἴνιγμα] 'A kind of riddle.'

ξυντιθέντι διαπειρωμένῳ] This interlacing of participles is not uncommon in Plato Cp. ἐξελθόντι . . . ἀμειβομένῳ, 37 D.

ἐμοῦ χαριεντιζομένου] For the genitive of a noun with participle after verbs of knowing, etc., see Riddell, Digest, § 26.

ὁ σοφὸς δή] δή shows that the epithet preceding is bestowed ironically. These finer touches have to be conveyed in English by the inflection of the voice.

ἐν τῷ εἰωθότι τρόπῳ] That is, by the use of the Socratic induction, which he now proceeds to apply.

καὶ μὴ ἄλλα καὶ ἄλλα θορυβείτω] 'And not be always raising some fresh disturbance.'

τὸ ἐπὶ τούτῳ γε] 'The next question at all events,' i. e. the question to which the induction had been intended to lead up. Cp. Gorg 512 E, τὸ ἐπὶ τούτῳ σκεπτέον, unless that be merely adverbial, as Cope takes it—'hereupon.' More usually the phrase is τὸ μετὰ τοῦτο Cp. Crat 391 B, Οὐκοῦν τὸ μετὰ τοῦτο χρὴ ζητεῖν: Prot. 355 A, τὸ μετὰ τοῦτο ἀκούετε: Crito 49 E.

C Ὡς ὤνησας] 'How kind of you'

ὑπὸ τουτωνὶ ἀναγκαζόμενος] See note on Καί μοι δεῦρο κ.τ.λ. 24 C.

διωμόσω] See note on ἀντωμοσία, 19 B.

ἀντιγραφῇ] Like ἀντωμοσία this term properly signifies the defendant's plea, but its meaning has been extended so as to cover the indictment Cp. note on ἀντωμοσία, 19 B.

τίθημι γάρ σε ὁμολογοῦντα κ.τ.λ] The saying 'silence gives consent' seems to have had its origin as one of the rules of the game of dialectic Cp Aristotle, Sophist Elench 5. § 13, ὁμολογοῦσι τῷ μὴ ἀποκρίνεσθαι τὸ ἐρωτώμενον; Cic. De Inv I, § 54.

D δαίμονας] On the nature and office of daemons, see a passage in the Symposium, 202 E-203 A. They were regarded as something intermediate between God and man, καὶ γὰρ πᾶν τὸ δαιμόνιον μεταξύ ἐστι θεοῦ τε καὶ θνητοῦ—the sources of all divination and prophecy, and the agents in the production of the supernatural generally The following is the definition of daemons given by Apuleius, who professed himself a follower of Plato, 'genere animalia, animo passiva, mente rationalia, corpore aeria, tempore aeterna' (Quoted by St Augustine, De Civ Dei IX 8) By the Jews daemons were considered to be the spirits of the wicked dead See Josephus, Bell Jud VII. 6. § 3 Hesiod, on the other hand, declared that they were the souls of the men of the golden age, Works and Days, 120-3—

αὐτὰρ ἐπειδὴ τοῦτο γένος κατὰ γαῖα κάλυψεν,
τοὶ μὲν δαίμονες εἰσὶ Διὸς μεγάλου διὰ βουλάς,
ἐσθλοί, ἐπιχθόνιοι, φύλακες θνητῶν ἀνθρώπων

In the Alcestis of Euripides 1002-4 we find the belief indicated that such a transformation was possible, at least in the heroic ages—

αὕτα ποτὲ προὔθαν᾽ ἀνδρός.
νῦν δ᾽ ἐστὶ μάκαιρα δαίμων
χαῖρ᾽, ὦ πότνι᾽, εὖ δὲ δοίης.

φάναι] Epexegetical of αἰνίττεσθαι καὶ χαριεντίζεσθαι

ἔκ τινων ἄλλων ὧν κ.τ.λ.] Translate—'by some other mothers, by whom, as you know, they are declared to be' It is tempting to take ἔκ τινων ἄλλων ὧν with Riddell as equivalent to ἐξ ἄλλων ὧν τινων, 'by whatsoever other mothers:' but probably we have nothing more here than the rather common omission of the preposition with the relative, when the antecedent has already been used with the same preposition. E g. Xen Conv. IV. § 1, ἐγὼ γὰρ ἐν τῷ χρόνῳ ᾧ ὑμῶν ἀκούω.

τοὺς ἡμιόνους] Both sense and sound are improved by the omission of these words, which are very likely due to some unintelligent commentator

τὴν γραφὴν ταύτην] These words again look like a marginal explanation of ταῦτα, which has crept into the text. It seems harsh to take ταῦτα as governed by ἀποπειρώμενος.

ὡς οὐ τοῦ αὐτοῦ] Translate the whole sentence thus—'But that you should persuade anyone who has the least grain of sense, that it is possible for the same person to believe in things pertaining to divine beings and gods, and yet, on the other hand, not to believe in divine beings or gods or heroes, is absolutely inconceivable.' The οὐ, as Riddell says is irrational, being simply a confused anticipation of the coming negative in οὐδεμία.

If anyone thinks this explanation too bold, he can extract a meaning out of the words as they stand, while allowing οὐ its proper force—'But that you should persuade anyone who has the least grain of sense, that it is possible for a man to believe in things pertaining to divine beings and at the same time not to believe in things pertaining to gods, and again for the same person not to believe in divine beings or gods or heroes, is absolutely inconceivable.' In this case the reasoning would run thus—You admit that I believe in δαιμόνια, yet you deny that I believe in θεῖα, and, what is more absurd still, while admitting that I believe in δαιμόνια, you deny that I believe in δαίμονες or in any other kind of supernatural personal agent.

ταῦτα] 'What you have heard.' Cp. note on 17 C, τῇδε τῇ 28 A ἡλικίᾳ

διαβολή] See note on 19 C, διαβολήν.

πολλοὺς καὶ ἄλλους κ.τ.λ.] 'Many other good men too'

οὐδὲν δὲ δεινόν κ τ.λ.] 'Nor is there any fear of their stopping short at me.' The subject to στῇ is ἃ δή above. This sentence is interesting, as it perhaps gives us the key to the common construction with οὐ μή. Riddell quotes Phaedo 84 B, οὐδὲν δεινὸν μὴ φοβηθῇ and Gorg 520 D, οὐδὲν δεινὸν αὐτῷ μήποτε ἀδικηθῇ. But see note on 29 D, οὐ μὴ παύσωμαι.

ὅτου τι καὶ σμικρὸν ὄφελός ἐστιν] 'A man of any worth at all.' For other instances of this expletive use of καί see Riddell, Digest, § 132

οἵ τε ἄλλοι καί] 'And above all.'

APOLOGY, NOTES. 28 C–E.

παρά] The root meaning of παρά is 'by the side of,' whence it easily passes into the idea of comparison.

θεὸς οὖσα] The feminine form, θεά, is seldom used in classical Greek except in poetry. Sometimes however it is necessary for distinction, as in Symp. 219 C, μὰ θεούς, μὰ θεάς. Contrast the beginning of Demosth. de Cor., τοῖς θεοῖς εὔχομαι πᾶσι καὶ πάσαις

αὐτίκα γάρ τοι κ.τ.λ] Homer, Iliad XVIII 94–6—
Τὸν δ' αὖτε προσέειπε Θέτις κατὰ δάκρυ χέουσα.
'ὠκύμορος δή μοι, τέκος, ἔσσεαι, οἷ' ἀγορεύεις
αὐτίκα γάρ τοι ἔπειτα μεθ' Ἕκτορα πότμος ἑτοῖμος.'

D αὐτίκα, φησί, τεθναίην, κ τ.λ.] Iliad XVIII 98—
αὐτίκα τεθναίην, ἐπεὶ οὐκ ἄρ' ἔμελλον ἑταίρῳ
κτεινομένῳ ἐπαμῦναι κ.τ.λ

The speech of Achilles (98–126), which begins as above, is a peculiarly rambling one; but Plato has seized upon the gist of it

κορωνίσιν] The word in Homer (Il. XVIII. 104) is ἐτώσιον Both Plato and Aristotle make slips occasionally in quoting Homer from memory. In some cases of course it is possible that their text may have differed from ours

[ἡ] ἡγησάμενος] If the ἡ is genuine, the sentence begins as though the participle were about to be balanced by some such clause as κελεύοντος τοῦ ἄρχοντος, and that then the construction is suddenly changed, probably from a latent consciousness that there was some inconsistency between the passivity of a soldier who is assigned a post and the active construction ἑαυτὸν τάξῃ.

Ἐγὼ οὖν κ τ λ.] The construction of this sentence is very remarkable Reduced to its simplest form it amounts to this—' Now it would be a strange thing for me to have done (apodosis), if I were to desert the post which the God assigned me, for fear of death or anything else whatever (protasis) ' But the protasis is complicated by a contrast being drawn between the actual behaviour of Socrates towards his human commanders and his supposed behaviour towards his divine commander. This contrast is managed by two clauses, of which the former has a μέν both in the protasis and the apodosis, which is answered by a δέ in the protasis and apodosis of the latter For a similar arrangement of particles cp. Meno 94 C, οὐκοῦν δῆλον κ.τ.λ and Gorg. 512 A, εἰ μέν τις μεγάλοις κ τ λ

E ἐν Ποτιδαίᾳ] The Athenians were engaged in operations against Potidaea from 432 to the close of 430 B.C. In the Charmides (153 A, B) Socrates is represented as returning from the camp at Potidaea just after a battle From the Symposium (220 E) we learn that Socrates saved the life of Alcibiades at Potidaea, and afterwards resigned the prize of valour in his favour.

ἐν Ἀμφιπόλει] In 422 B.C. took place the battle at Amphipolis, in which both Brasidas and Cleon fell

ἐπὶ Δηλίῳ] After the disastrous defeat at Delium in B.C 424 Socrates and Laches retired from the field together. The look of dogged determination on Socrates' face served better than haste to protect him from the foe Alcibiades, who was on horseback, repaid his debt to Socrates and covered his retreat (Symp 221 A, B; Laches 181 B).

φιλοσοφοῦντά με δεῖν ζῆν] 'The duty of passing my life in the study of philosophy ' δεῖν here might fairly be called a cognate accusative after τάττοντος. It has a tendency to be used somewhat superfluously. Cp. 35 C, ἀξιοῦτέ με ... δεῖν.

ἀπειθῶν] The participles are explanatory of οὐ νομίζω θεοὺς εἶναι, **29 A** 'if I were disobedient,' etc Socrates still speaks as though the oracle had directly enjoined the eccentric course of life which he pursued Cp note on κατὰ τὸν θεόν, 22 A, and the words ζητῶ καὶ ἐρευνῶ κατὰ τὸν θεόν, 23 B

δοκεῖν σοφὸν εἶναι] 'Seeming to be wise.' Supply τινα. For its omission cp. Meno 81 D, ἀναμνησθέντα

καὶ ἐνταῦθα] ' In this matter also,' i. e. with regard to the fear **B** of death.

τούτῳ ἄν] Supply φαίην.

ὅτι οὐκ εἰδώς κ τ λ] 'That, having no adequate knowledge about the other world, I think also that I have not.'

ὧν οἶδα] Attraction of the Relative is most common in Greek when the antecedent is in the genitive, as here, or in the dative, and the relative in the accusative.

ἃ μὴ οἶδα] 'Things of which I cannot know.' The μή is due to the hypothetical character of the sentence—'If I am in doubt as to the nature of a thing, I will not fear it more than what I know to be evil.'

εἰ ἀγαθὰ ὄντα τυγχάνει] 'Whether they may not be good' This is a case in which English idiom requires a negative, while Greek does not.

ὥστε οὐδ' εἰ με νῦν] This sentence is one of extraordinary length. The protasis is repeated three times in different shapes, first in the indicative, which marks an objective contingency; (1) εἰ με οὖν ὑμεῖς ἀφίετε, and then twice over in the optative, which marks a subjective contingency, or a case contemplated as possible ; (2) εἰ μοι πρὸς ταῦτα εἴποιτε; (3) εἰ οὖν με, ὅπερ εἶπον, ἐπὶ τούτοις ἀφίοιτε ; the apodosis begins at εἴποιμ' ἂν ὑμῖν in D and ends at φροντίζεις in E.

τὴν ἀρχήν] 'At all.' **C**

ἐπειδὴ εἰσῆλθον] 'Now that I have been brought up.' Cp. note on 17 D, ἀναβέβηκα and on 26 A, ἐὰν μάθω.

ἄν . . . διαφθαρήσονται] For ἄν with the fut. indic. see Riddell, Digest, § 58.

ἐφ' ᾧτε μηκέτι . . διατρίβειν] For the infinitive after the relative cp Xen Hell II. 3 § 11, αἱρεθέντες δὲ ἐφ' ᾧτε συγγράψαι νόμους, and see Riddell, Digest, § 79.

D ἀσπάζομαι μὲν καὶ φιλῶ] 'I am your very humble servant' Literally 'I embrace and kiss you.' Somewhat similar is the use of ἐπαινῶ καὶ φιλῶ in Prot. 335 D.

πείσομαι δὲ μᾶλλον τῷ θεῷ ἢ ὑμῖν] Cp. Acts v 29, Πειθαρχεῖν δεῖ Θεῷ μᾶλλον ἢ ἀνθρώποις: also iv 19. Modern sentiment would incline us to render this simply 'God'; but probably it is meant for Apollo.

οὐ μὴ παύσωμαι] See note on 28 B, οὐδὲν δὲ δεινόν κ.τ.λ. Goodwin indeed Greek Grammar, § 257) declares that the double negative has merely the force of emphasis, and that the subjunctive is a relic of the old usage which we find in Homer, in which it is equivalent to a future.

Οὐ γάρ πω τοίους ἴδον ἀνέρας, οὐδὲ ἴδωμαι (II. I. 262).

χρημάτων μέν] χρήματα are the lowest form of external goods, δόξα καὶ τιμή the highest, φρόνησις and ἀλήθεια are internal goods which no one can take away or withhold.

30 A νεωτέρῳ] Dative of advantage.

ἐγγυτέρω] This predicative use of the adverb makes it really an indeclinable adjective.

B οὐκ ἐκ χρημάτων κ.τ.λ] The conduciveness of virtue to material prosperity is incontestable as regards a community. The difficulty is to persuade the individual that virtue is conducive to his personal welfare, which, as he conceives of it, is not always the case. The material advantages of virtue are insisted on by Socrates in the Memorabilia. See for instance the conversation with Aristippus (II. 1) on the advantages of self-control. Cp. Arist. Pol. VII. 1. § 6

ταῦτ' ἂν εἴη βλαβερά] 'That, I grant you, would be mischievous.'

C ἐμμείνατέ μοι] 'Abide, pray' Ethic dative.

ἄττα] Neut. pl. of the indefinite pronoun; to be distinguished from ἅττα = ἅ ἅττα), neut. pl. of ὅστις.

οὐκ ἐμὲ μείζω βλάψετε κ.τ.λ.] 'You will not be doing so much harm to me as to yourselves.' Another instance of the ineradicable εἰρωνεία of Attic diction. Cp. note on 19 A, καὶ οὐ πάνυ κ.τ.λ.

ἂν βλάψειαν] 'Is not likely to hurt me.' Attic future.

δύναιτο] Singular, because οὔτε Μέλητος οὔτε Ἄνυτος is dis- D junctive.

θεμιτόν] 'Permitted by the divine law' Latin *fas*.

ἀποκτείνειε] Notice the Aeolic form of the aorist in this and the two verbs which follow.

ἀτιμώσειεν] This has been substituted on the authority of Stobaeus for the common reading ἀτιμάσειεν. Ἀτιμάζω properly means to treat as ἄτιμος, ἀτιμόω to make ἄτιμος

πολὺ μᾶλλον] Supply μέγα κακὸν οἴομαι εἶναι

πολλοῦ δέω] The usual construction with πολλοῦ δεῖν is with the simple infinitive as here. Cp. below 35 D, 37 B; Meno 79 B, αὐτὴν μὲν πολλοῦ δεῖς εἰπεῖν ὅ τι ἔστι, 92 A, πολλοῦ γε δέουσι μαίνεσθαι.

ἀλλ᾽ ὑπὲρ ὑμῶν] ' No, it is on your behalf ' Supply some word like λέγω from ἀπολογεῖσθαι

εἰ καὶ γελοιότερον εἰπεῖν] There is an ellipse of δεῖ or some E such word Cp Gorg. 486 C, εἴ τι καὶ ἀγροικότερον εἰρῆσθαι

μύωπος] From its proper meaning of ' gadfly,' which it has here, μύωψ passed by a very intelligible transition to that of a ' spur,' which it bears in Theophrastus (Charact V (λxi) Tauchnitz), ἐν τοῖς μύωψι ἐς τὴν ἀγορὰν περιπατεῖν.

προστεθεικέναι] The active, of which προσκείμενον preceding is the passive. See note on ἐὰν μάθω, 26 A.

προσκαθίζων] 'Settling upon' The metaphor of the gadfly is 31 A still continued

ὑμεῖς δ᾽ ἴσως τάχ᾽ ἄν] The τάχ᾽ ἄν merely reinforces ἴσως ' But you perhaps might be apt in a rage,' etc.

κρούσαντες] 'With a tap' Hermann has substituted on his own conjecture ὁρούσαντες, which would mean 'having made a rush at me.'

τῶν οἰκείων] This refers to affairs which touched his family, as B distinguished from those which were purely personal Xanthippe had her grievances.

ὥσπερ πατέρα κ τ.λ.] In the accusative because of the ἐμέ preceding. ' As a father or an elder brother might.'

τοῦτό γε κ.τ λ.] ' Could not carry their shamelessness to such a pitch as to adduce a witness.' The force of the sentence lies in the participial clause. See Riddell, Digest, § 303, and cp. 31 D

ἱκανόν . . . ἐγὼ παρέχομαι τὸν μάρτυρα] See note on οὐ γὰρ C ἐμὸν ἐρῶ τὸν λόγον, 20 E.

τὴν πενίαν] See note on 23 B, ἐν πενίᾳ μυρίᾳ.

ἀναβαίνων] See note on ἀναβέβηκα, 17 D. Riddell explains the word differently in this passage, taking it to refer to the Pnyx, ' as in the famous πᾶς ὁ δῆμος ἄνω καθῆτο, Dem. de Cor. 169, p. 285.'

D **θεῖόν τι καὶ δαιμόνιον**] See Introduction

ὃ δὴ καί κ τ.λ] 'Which in fact is the thing that Meletus was poking fun at in his indictment, when he drew it up' For the force of the participle see note on 31 D above, τοῦτό γε κ τ λ, and for the fact cp Euthyphro 3 B

ἐπικωμῳδῶν] We have διακωμῳδεῖν used in the Gorgias, 462 E, μὴ οἴηταί με διακωμῳδεῖν τὸ ἑαυτοῦ ἐπιτήδευμα

τοῦτ' ἐστίν . ἀρξάμενον]. See Introduction, p. 11.

τοῦτ' ἔστιν ὅ μοι ἐναντιοῦται κ τ.λ] Cp Rep 496 C

ἀπολώλη] Notice the Attic forms of the pluperfect, ἀπολώλη and ὠφελήκη contracted from the old termination in -εα So ἀνεστήκη in Prot 335 D

32 A **ἰδιωτεύειν ἀλλὰ μὴ δημοσιεύειν**] Verbs in -ευω formed from nouns, whether substantive or adjective, denote being in the state expressed by the noun

τεκμήρια παρέξομαι κ τ λ] 'Here appears, in a refined form, the common τύπος of rehearsing a man's past services in his defence' Riddell

οὐδ' ἂν ἑνί] The separation of οὐδέ or μηδέ from εἷς renders the expression more emphatic. Cp Gorg 521 C, "Ως μοι δοκεῖς, ὦ Σώκρατες, πιστεύειν μηδ' ἂν ἐν τούτων παθεῖν

ὑπεικάθοιμι] Cp. Soph El. 361 This form is considered by many authorities, including Liddell and Scott, to be a second aorist of ὑπείκω, resembling ἔσχεθον lengthened from ἔσχον Cp ἐδιώκαθες, Gorg 483 A.

μὴ ὑπείκων δὲ ἅμα κ τ λ] The first ἅμα goes with ὑπείκων, the second with ἀπολοίμην. 'And, rather than yield, would be ready to perish on the spot' Cp. Hom. Od. XI. 371; Eur. Hel. 587.

δικανικά] 'I will tell you a vulgar story and one which smacks of the law-courts, but which is nevertheless true.' Cp. note on τεκμήρια παρέξομαι κ τ λ above

B **ἄλλην μὲν ἀρχήν**] 'Though I never held any office at all in the city, yet I was a member of council'

['Ἀντιοχίς] This word may be a gloss, but there would be nothing surprising in the omission of the article with the proper name: cp Meno 70 B, οἱ τοῦ σοῦ ἑταίρου Ἀριστίππου πολῖται Λαρισαῖοι, and Phaedo 57 A. τῶν πολιτῶν Φλιασίων

τοὺς δέκα στρατηγούς] The circumstances attending this famous trial are related by Xenophon in his Hellenics (I chs 4–7) Alcibiades after his triumphant return to Athens in B.C. 407 soon lost the popularity which had led to his being appointed sole commander of the Athenian forces (ἁπάντων ἡγεμὼν αὐτοκράτωρ) He was deposed, and in his place ten generals were appointed, namely,

Conon, Diomedon, Leon, Pericles, Erasinides, Aristocrates, Archestratus, Protomachus, Thrasyllus, Aristogenes In the following year, B C 406, Conon, Leon, and Erasinides were besieged in Mitylene by the Spartan commander, Callicratidas. Diomedon made an ineffectual attempt to relieve them with twelve ships, of which ten were instantly captured. Then the Athenians put to sea with all their forces, and came to the rescue with 120 ships. Their squadron lay at Arginusae, some islands off the coast of Lesbos, where Callicratidas offered them battle, with a fleet of inferior numbers The result was a great victory for the Athenians, who captured about 70 of the enemy's ships, at a loss of 25 of their own. The Athenian commanders during this action were the following eight—Aristocrates, Diomedon, Pericles, Erasinides, Protomachus, Thrasyllus, Lysias, Aristogenes Seven of these names are the same as before. Conon was still besieged in Mitylene by 50 vessels which had been left by Callicratidas under the charge of Eteonicus Leon, we may conjecture, had been captured in attempting to bring news of Conon's situation to Athens (see I. 6 § 21) Lysias may have been sent from Athens to supply his place Xenophon makes no further mention of Archestratus · but we know that he died at Mitylene (Lysias, 'Απολ. Δωροδ. p. 162; Bekker, vol. I. p. 331). After the battle the Athenian commanders decided in council that 47 vessels should be left under the command of Theramenes, Thrasybulus, and others, to pick up the survivors off twelve of their own ships, which had been water-logged by the enemy, while they themselves proceeded to attack the besieging force under Eteonicus at Mitylene. A great storm which ensued prevented either of these operations from being carried out.

The Athenians at home were not satisfied with the conduct of the commanders, and deposed them all except Conon, whose situation had exempted him from blame. Of the eight who were engaged in the battle, two—Protomachus and Aristogenes—did not return to Athens. The remaining six—Pericles, Diomedon, Lysias, Aristocrates, Thrasyllus, and Erasinides—found themselves on their return the objects of popular odium, one of the foremost of their accusers being Theramenes, the very man whose duty it had been, according to their statement, to attend to the recovery of the missing sailors. Sentimental appeals were made to the passions of an excitable populace, and at last a senator named Callixenus was induced to propose that the generals should be tried in a body, and, if found guilty, should be put to death. Some of the prytanes refused at first to put this motion to the vote, as being illegal, but they were frightened into compliance, with the single exception of Socrates.

The opposition of Socrates, however, though dignified, was ultimately useless. Sentence of death was passed on the eight generals, and the six who were present were executed. *Menexenus* 243 C, D shows the strength of the popular sentiment with regard to this passage in history.

ναυμαχίας] The battle of Arginusae.

παρανόμως] They were entitled each to a separate trial, and they had not been allowed a fair hearing (Xen. Hell. I. 7 § 5, οἱ στρατηγοὶ βραχέως ἕκαστος ἀπελογήσατο, οὐ γὰρ προὐτέθη σφίσι λόγος κατὰ τὸν νόμον·

ὡς ἐν τῷ ὑστέρῳ χρόνῳ] It was not long before the Athenians repented of their precipitate action. Proceedings were taken against Callixenus and others who had been prominent in procuring the condemnation of the generals; but they effected their escape during a tumult before they were brought to trial. Callixenus returned to Athens in B.C. 403, when the people came back from the Piraeus, but he was universally detested, and died of starvation (Xen. Hell. I. 7 § 34.

ἠναντιώθην [ὑμῖν] μηδὲν ποιεῖν] 'Opposed your doing anything contrary to the laws.' The negative is due to the expression being proleptic. The tendency of the opposition was to make the people do nothing unlawful. The idiom of the French language is in these cases similar to that of the Greek: 'J' empêchais que vous ne fissiez rien contre les lois'

This incident in the career of Socrates is referred to, with the usual delicate irony with which Plato invests his character, in *Gorgias* 473 E, Ὦ Πῶλε, οὐκ εἰμὶ τῶν πολιτικῶν, καὶ πέρυσι βουλεύειν λαχών, ἐπειδὴ ἡ φυλὴ ἐπρυτάνευε, καὶ ἔδει με ἐπιψηφίζειν, γέλωτα παρεῖχον καὶ οὐκ ἠπιστάμην ἐπιψηφίζειν. References to the same transaction will be found in *Axiochus* 368 D, E; Xen. *Mem* I 1. § 18; IV. 4. § 2. In both passages of the Memorabilia it is distinctly stated that Socrates was *ἐπιστάτης* on the occasion. We learn from the passage in the Axiochus that the opponents of the generals carried their point next day by means of a packed committee, οἱ δὲ περὶ Θηραμένην καὶ Καλλίξενον τῇ ὑστεραίᾳ προέδρους ἐγκαθέτους ὑφέντες κατεχειροτόνησαν τῶν ἀνδρῶν ἄκριτον θάνατον.

[*καὶ ἐναντία ἐψηφισάμην*] These words are suspected of being a gloss. The way in which Socrates opposed the popular will was by refusing to put the question to the vote at all, which in his capacity of chairman (*ἐπιστάτης*) it lay with him to do. Riddell accepts the words, and refers them by a *hysteron proteron* to Socrates voting in committee against the bill being laid before the people.

ἐνδεικνύναι με καὶ ἀπάγειν] 'To inform against me or have me summarily arrested.' ἀνάγειν in Baiter's text seems to be due to a misprint.

φοβηθέντα δεσμὸν ἢ θάνατον] Callixenus threatened to have the C recalcitrant prytanes included in the same vote with the generals. Xen. Hell I. 7. § 14.

ἐπειδὴ δὲ ὀλιγαρχία ἐγένετο] This was in B C. 404, a year which was known in Athenian history as 'the anarchy.' Xen. Hell II 3. § 1

οἱ τριάκοντα] The names of the Thirty may be read in Xen. Hell. II. 3. § 2. The leading spirit among them was Critias. They were chosen by the people, under the auspices of Lysander, with the ostensible object of codifying the laws of Athens

πέμπτον αὐτόν] 'With four others.' The beautiful conciseness of this idiom has been imitated in the French language. See, for instance, Voltaire, Siècle de Lous XIV, ch. 12: 'Il échappe à peine lui quatrième'

τὴν θόλον] The Dome or Rotunda, a building shaped like the Radcliffe, in which the Prytanes dined, and the Scribes also (Demosthenes, De Fals Leg p 419 ad fin.). It was near the council-chamber of the Five Hundred See Pausanias I. 5. § 1, τοῦ βουλευτηρίου τῶν πεντακοσίων πλησίον Θόλος ἐστὶ καλουμένη, καὶ θύουσί τε ἐνταῦθα οἱ πρυτάνεις

Notice that the gender of θόλος is feminine, like that of so many words of the second declension which convey the idea of a cavity, e g χηλύς, κιβωτός, τάφρος.

Λέοντα τὸν Σαλαμίνιον] A man of reputation and capacity, who had been guilty of no crime Xen Hell. II. 3. § 39. Cp. Mem. IV 4 § 3.

ἀναπλῆσαι] 'To implicate.' Lit to infect. Cp. Phaedo 83 D, τοῦ σώματος ἀναπλέα; Ai Acharn. 847, δικῶν ἀναπλήσει.

ἀγροικότερον] 'Too clownish' The opposite of ἀγροῖκος is D ἀστεῖος, which implies refinement and breeding. For the phrase εἰ μὴ ἀγροικότερον ἦν εἰπεῖν cp. Euthyd. 283 E.

τούτου δὲ τὸ πᾶν μέλει] 'This, I say, is all my care.' δέ here lends emphasis to the τούτου. This use of δέ should be compared with its employment in the combination καὶ . . δέ.

διὰ ταχέων κατελύθη] They were deposed before the end of the E year and a body of ten men, one from each tribe, elected in their place. Xen. Hell II. 4. § 23

μαθητάς] 'Xenophon in his Memorabilia speaks always of the 33 A companions of Socrates, not of his disciples· οἱ συνόντες αὐτῷ, οἱ συνουσιασταί (I. 6. § 1)—οἱ συνδιατρίβοντες—οἱ συγγιγνόμενοι—οἱ ἑταῖροι—οἱ ὁμιλοῦντες αὐτῷ—οἱ συνήθεις (IV 8. § 2)—οἱ μεθ' ἑαυτοῦ (IV. 2. § 1 ad fin.)—οἱ ἐπιθυμηταί I. 2 § 60). Aristippus also, in speaking to Plato, talked of Socrates as ὁ ἑταῖρος ἡμῶν. Aristot Rhetor II. 24.' Grote's History of Greece, vol VIII. p. 212, note 3, ed of 1884. We may add to this list the term ὁμιλητής, Mem I. 2. §§ 12, 48.

ἐγὼ δὲ διδάσκαλος κ τ λ.] Cp. Xen Mem. I 2. § 3, Καίτοι γε οὐδεπώποτε ὑπέσχετο διδάσκαλος εἶναι τούτου (i e. τοῦ καλοὺς καὶ ἀγαθοὺς εἶναι).

τὰ ἐμαυτοῦ πράττοντος] That is, carrying out his divine mission. Cp. 28 E; 29 D above; 33 C below In the Gorgias Socrates is made to say that the soul which is most likely to please Rhadamanthys is that which has inhabited the body φιλοσόφου τὰ αὐτοῦ πράξαντος καὶ οὐ πολυπραγμονήσαντος ἐν τῷ βίῳ

οὐδὲ χρήματα μὲν λαμβάνων κ τ.λ.] On this subject see Xen. Mem. I. 2 §§ 5–7 and § 60, οὐδένα πώποτε μισθὸν τῆς συνουσίας ἐπράξατο, ἀλλὰ πᾶσιν ἀφθόνως ἐπήρκει τῶν ἑαυτοῦ. also I 5 § 6 Cp note on 19 E, χρήματα πράττομαι

B   ἐρωτᾶν] 'To ask him questions'

καὶ ἐάν τις κ τ λ.] This is a soft way of saying, 'And I am ready to question him, if he chooses.' Riddell

οὐκ ἂν δικαίως τὴν αἰτίαν ὑπέχοιμι] Among the followers of Socrates had been Critias and Alcibiades, about the two most unprincipled men of their time This point was urged against him on the trial. See Xen Mem. I. 2 §§ 12–18

C   εἶπον, ὅτι.] With a comma at εἶπον, ὅτι is explanatory of πᾶσαν τὴν ἀλήθειαν, 'I told you the whole truth, how that they take pleasure,' etc. But with a colon at εἶπον, ὅτι will mean 'because,' and convey the answer to the question with which the sentence begins, 'It is because they take pleasure,' etc. Cp Euthyphro 3 B.

ἐμοὶ δὲ τοῦτο κ τ λ.] The intense belief in his own divine mission, which is here so emphatically expressed, is one of the chief factors to be taken into account in estimating the character of Socrates.

θεία μοῖρα] 'Divine dispensation'

D   ἔγνωσαν] 'Had found out.' See note on ἔγνωκας, 25 D.

ἀναβαίνοντας] See note on ἀναβέβηκα, 17 D

τινάς] The construction of accusative and infinitive after χρῆν is still continued.

ὑπ' ἐμοῦ] See note on πεπόνθατε ὑπό, 17 A.

πάρεισιν . ἐνταυθοῖ] An instance of compressed construction, or *constructio praegnans*, 'Are present hither' = 'Have come hither and are present here.'

Κρίτων] The attachment of Crito to Socrates is very touching. Crito was a wealthy man, apparently engaged in business (Euthyd. 304 C), who was always ready to place his riches at the disposal of his friend (38 B; Crito 45 B). It was Crito who made arrangements for Socrates' escape from prison, and who affectionately urged him to avail himself of them; it was Crito who received his last behest, and who closed his eyes in death (Phaedo 118 A). He was the author of a book containing seventeen dialogues on thoroughly Socratic subjects. The titles of them may be read in Diogenes Laertius II. § 121. According to this author Crito had four sons, Critobulus, Hermogenes, Epigenes, Ctesippus, who were all instructed by Socrates. It would appear, however, from Euthyd 306 D, that he had only two, Critobulus and another who was considerably younger. This may be due to the supposed date of the dialogue. But more probably the statement of Diogenes is erroneous Hermogenes, Epigenes, and Ctesippus are present in the Phaedo (59 B) along with Critobulus, which may have led to the error

ἐμὸς ἡλικιώτης] This renders improbable the statement given on E the authority of Demetrius of Byzantium that Crito took Socrates away from his trade and educated him, being struck with his ability (Diog. Laert. II § 20 ad fin.)

δημότης] Socrates belonged to the deme of Alopece

Κριτοβούλου] See note on Κρίτων above. Also Phaedo 59 B. The conduct of Critobulus is made the text of a sermon from Socrates in the Memorabilia, I 3 §§ 8-15, cp II. 6 §§ 31, 32. His appearance as a boy is described in Euthyd 271 B He figures in the Œconomicus and in the Symposium of Xenophon He appears to have excited the animosity of Aeschines the Socratic

Λυσανίας ὁ Σφήττιος] Nothing is known of Lysanias, the father of Aeschines, beyond what we learn from this passage. He is to be distinguished from Lysanias, the father of Cephalus, Rep 330 B. We may set aside on the authority of Plato the statement to which Diogenes Laertius (II § 60) inclines, that Aeschines was the son of Charinus, a sausage-maker.

Αἰσχίνου] Commonly known as 'Aeschines the Socratic' (Cic. De Inv I 31; Athen. V 220 a, XIII. 611 e). He was one of the most prominent among the immediate disciples of Socrates, and is mentioned in the Phaedo (59 B) as having been present at the death of his master. A collection of dialogues went under his name in antiquity, of which Diogenes (II. §§ 60, 61) sets aside several as spurious. Scandal declared that the remainder were really the works of Socrates himself, which had been given to Aeschines by Xanthippe after the death of the philosopher Athen. XIII. 611 e, ὡς οἱ ἀμφὶ τὸν Ἰδομενία φασίν Cp Diog. Laert. II § 60, where the same thing is asserted on the authority of Menedemus of Eretria). Even his friend Aristippus is said to have exclaimed against him as a plagiarist when he heard him give a public reading at Megara (Diog Laert. II. § 62 ad fin.). Aeschines seems to have been embarrassed all his life by poverty, possibly on account of an inclination to good living; for Socrates recommended him 'to borrow from himself, by decreasing his diet' (Diog. Laert. II. § 62). After the death of Socrates he set up as a perfumer, but became bankrupt. The tirade of Lysias the orator against him, a fragment of which has been preserved by Athenaeus (XIII. 611 e–612 f) represents his conduct at this time as most degraded. Driven to seek his fortune in Sicily, he was neglected by Plato, but welcomed by Aristippus, who introduced him at the court of Dionysius, from whom he received presents in return for his dialogues. He is said to have stayed at Syracuse until the expulsion of the tyrant. On his return to Athens he did not venture to enter into rivalry with the schools of Plato and Aristippus, but gave lectures for pay, and composed speeches for the law-courts. In his style he chiefly imitated Gorgias of Leontium. There is an amusing instance of inductive reasoning quoted from his works by Cicero (De Inv I. 31), in which Aspasia a Socrates in petticoats, gives a moral lesson to Xenophon and his wife.

Ἀντιφῶν ὁ Κηφισιεύς] To be distinguished from the Antiphon of the Parmenides (126 B), who was the son of Pyrilampes and half-brother to Plato; also from Antiphon the Sophist, who figures in the Memorabilia I. 6, and who may be the same with Antiphon the Rhamnusian of Menexenus, 236 A.

Ἐπιγένους] Epigenes is mentioned as present at the death of Socrates (Phaedo 59 B). In the Memorabilia III. 12 we find Socrates remonstrating with him on the neglect of bodily exercise

ἐν ταύτῃ τῇ διατριβῇ γεγόνασι] 'Have been in this way of living.' The word came to be used later for 'a school'

Νικόστρατος] There is an actor of this name mentioned by Xenophon (Conv. VI § 3); but we have no reason to suppose that he is the same person.

ὥστε . . καταδεηθείη] 'So that he at least could not bring any improper influence to bear upon him.' ἐκεῖνος refers to Theodotus, αὐτοῦ to Nicostratus.

Πάραλος] Distinguish this person from Paralus, the son of Pericles, for whom see Alc. 118 E; Prot. 315 A; Meno 94 B.

34 A Δημοδόκου] In the Theages Demodocus is represented as bringing to Socrates his son Theages, who has an ambition to become σοφός

Θεάγης] In Rep 496 B, C, Socrates speaks of 'his friend Theages' being only prevented by ill-health from abandoning philosophy for politics He gives his name to the dialogue above mentioned.

Ἀδείμαντος] This brother of Plato's appears both in the Parmenides (126 A) and in the Republic (see especially 362 D - 367 E). The genius and virtue of himself and his brother Glaucon are extolled by Socrates, who quotes from an elegiac tribute of some admirer of Glaucon's (368 A)—

παῖδες Ἀρίστωνος, κλεινοῦ θεῖον γένος ἀνδρός.

Πλάτων] There are only three passages in all the works of Plato in which he names himself, namely, the one before us, 38 B, and Phaedo 59 B, where it is mentioned that he was ill at the time of the death of Socrates.

Ἀπολλόδωρος] Of Phalerum (Symp. 172 A). Mentioned in the Phaedo as having been specially affected by grief during his last interview with Socrates (59 A ad fin , 117 D). He is the supposed narrator of the dialogue in the Symposium. His devotion to Socrates and to philosophy was that of a religious enthusiast, and procured him the surname of 'the madman' (Symp 172, 173). Xenophon speaks of him as ἐπιθυμητὴς μὲν ἰσχυρῶς αὐτοῦ (i.e. Σωκράτους), ἄλλως δ' εὐηθής (Apol. Soc § 28).

ἐν τῷ ἑαυτοῦ λόγῳ] 'In his own time of speaking,' as measured by the κλεψύδρα, or water-clock. Cp. the expression of Demosthenes (De Cor. p 274), ἐν τῷ ἐμῷ ὕδατι The water was stopped while witnesses were speaking.

ἐγὼ παραχωρῶ] Riddell quotes from Aeschines (In Ctes. p. 77) the full expression, παραχωρῶ σοι τοῦ βήματος, ἕως ἂν εἴπῃς.

ταῦτα καὶ .. τοιαῦτα] Οὗτος, being the demonstrative of the C second person, is appropriately used of what has gone before, and is now in possession of the hearer. Translate ταῦτα 'what you have heard.' See note on τῇδε τῇ ἡλικίᾳ, 17 C

εἰ ὁ μέν] 'How that he'

τὴν ψῆφον] Words of the second declension that denote earths, D stones, and the like are generally feminine Cp. note on τὴν θόλον, 32 C.

οὐκ ἀξιῶ μὲν γάρ] (I say 'if') for, etc.

λέγειν λέγων] Where similar words have to be used in the same sentence Plato always prefers to bring them together. We have a remarkable instance in C above, ἀγῶνος ἀγῶνα ἀγωνιζόμενος. See also note on 19 B, διέβαλλον οἱ διαβάλλοντες.

APOLOGY. NOTES. 34 D–36 A.

τὸ τοῦ Ὁμήρου] Od XIX. 163—
οὐ γὰρ ἀπὸ δρυός ἐσσι παλαιφάτου οὐδ' ἀπὸ πέτρης.

εἰς μὲν μειράκιον κ.τ.λ.] Cp Phaedo 116 B, δύο γὰρ αὐτῷ υἱεῖς σμικροὶ ἦσαν, εἷς δὲ μέγας. The name of the eldest was Lamprocles (Xen. Mem II. 2. § 1). The two youngest were Sophroniscus and Menexenus (Diog Laert. II. 26).

E **τηλικόνδε**] See note on 25 D, τηλικούτου ὄντος κ.τ λ We may translate, if it be not over-refinement, 'At my time of life, and with the reputation you know of'

διαφέρειν] This word is constantly used by the figure meiosis in the sense of 'to be superior'

B **ταῖς ἄλλαις τιμαῖς**] 'Other posts of distinction' Like *honores* in Latin.

τὰ ἐλεεινὰ ταῦτα δράματα] 'These harrowing stage-effects'

C **ἐπὶ τούτῳ**] 'For this purpose' Cp ψεύδεται καὶ ἐπὶ διαβολῇ τῇ ἐμῇ λέγει.

ἐθίζεσθαι] 'Let yourselves be accustomed' An instance of what Riddell calls the semi-middle sense of the verb See Digest § 88 Both passive and middle tenses are so used Cp Meno 91 C, λωβηθῆναι.

ἀξιοῦτέ με . . . δεῖν] 'Expect that I ought' See note on 28 E, φιλοσοφοῦντά με δεῖν ζῆν, and cp Gorg 512 C, παρακαλῶν ἐπὶ τὸ δεῖν γίγνεσθαι μηχανοποιούς.

D **ἄλλως τε κ.τ.λ.**] A violent tmesis The words μέντοι νὴ Δία are thrust into the middle of the phrase ἄλλως τε πάντως καί See Riddell's note.

φεύγοντα ὑπό] See note on πεπόνθατε ὑπό, 17 A

κατηγοροίην] Notice that vowel verbs take this Attic form of the optative in preference to the usual termination in -οιμι

τῷ θεῷ] See note on 19 B.

E **τὸ μὲν μὴ ἀγανακτεῖν**] This substantival clause is the direct object after ξυμβάλλεται, just as we might have ξυμβάλλεσθαι χρήματα, ἱμάτια, etc.

A **γέγονε τὸ γεγονὸς τοῦτο**] See note on 19 B, διέβαλλον οἱ διαβάλλοντες.

οὕτω παρ' ὀλίγον] 'So close a thing.' παρ' ὀλίγον is treated as one expression, so that the οὕτω precedes.

εἰ τριάκοντα μόναι κ.τ λ] Riddell, following Heffter, takes the total number of Socrates' judges to have been 501. Then, accepting the statement of Diogenes Laertius (II. § 41), that the majority against Socrates was 281, as representing the aggregate of condemning votes, he draws the conclusion that the minority in his favour must have consisted of 220. For 31 votes exactly, or 30 in round numbers, would thus suffice to turn the scale. It appears that a Heliastic court always consisted of one more than some multiple of 100, the odd man being thrown in to prevent an equality of votes. See Riddell's Introduction, pp. xii–xiv.

ἀποπεφεύγη] Notice the omission of the augment, for which cp. ὡς ἐν τῇ γραφῇ γέγραπτο, Xen. Mem. I. 2. § 64

παντὶ δῆλον τοῦτό γε κ τ.λ.] A fallacy which is not intended to deceive, in other words, a jest Socrates playfully assumes that as there were three accusers, each of them ought to be credited with one-third of the votes. As these amounted altogether only to 281, Meletus could not claim a full hundred, which was the fifth part required out of the total of 501.

ἀνέβησαν] See note on ἀναβέβηκα, 17 D.

χιλίας δραχμάς] See the law quoted in Demosthenes against Meidias, p 529, ὅσοι δ' ἂν γράφωνται γραφὰς ἰδίας κατὰ τὸν νόμον, ἐάν τις μὴ ἐπεξέλθῃ ἢ ἐπεξιὼν μὴ μεταλάβῃ τὸ πέμπτον μέρος τῶν ψήφων, ἀποτισάτω χιλίας δραχμὰς τῷ δημοσίῳ

τιμᾶται . θανάτου] Cp end of note on 24 B, Σωκράτη φησὶν ἀδικεῖν

ὑμῖν] Ethic dative 'And whereat would you have me set the counter-assessment?'

παθεῖν ἢ ἀποτῖσαι] A reference to the terms of the law above quoted in the note on χιλίας δραχμάς. See again Demosthenes against Meidias, p 529—ὅτου δ' ἂν καταγνῷ ἡ ἡλικία, τιμάτω περὶ αὐτοῦ παραχρῆμα, ὅτου ἂν δοκῇ ἄξιος εἶναι παθεῖν ἢ ἀποτῖσαι. παθεῖν means suffering in person, ἀποτῖσαι in pocket. The phrase passed into use in conversation See Xen. Conv V. § 8.

ὅ τι μαθών] The indirect form of the phrase, τί μαθών, which like τί παθών may loosely be rendered 'Wherefore?' But there is this original difference between the two, that τί μαθών must have referred to reasoned and voluntary action, τί παθών to involuntary, 'What ails you that?' See Arist. Acharn. 826:—

τί δὴ μαθὼν φαίνεις ἄνευ θρυαλλίδος,
On what principle do you shine without a wick?
(The pun is untranslateable.)

For the indirect form of the phrase, cp Euthyd. 283 E, σοὶ εἰς κεφαλήν, ὅ τι μαθών μου καὶ τῶν ἄλλων καταψεύδει τοιοῦτο πρᾶγμα, and again 299 A, πολὺ μέντοι, ἔφη, δικαιότερον τὸν ὑμέτερον πατέρα τύπτοιμι, ὅ τι μαθὼν σοφοὺς υἱεῖς οὕτως ἔφυσεν The phrase appears to have passed so completely into a mere formula as to admit of being used even in the neuter plural. See Prot 353 D (where Hermann has altered the reading on his own conjecture into ὅτι παρόντα'. Translate here, ' In that, for whatsoever reason, I allowed myself no rest in the disposal of my life'

τῶν ἄλλων ἀρχῶν] Notice the idiomatic use of ἄλλων All the things previously mentioned do not come under the head of what follows ἄλλων, as the word 'other' would imply in English. The force of ἄλλων extends to all three genitives which follow Translate 'and what not besides—official posts and political clubs and the factions that go on in the city' See Riddell's note and Digest, § 46, and cp Meno 92 B. A good instance of the idiom in question is to be found in Gorg. 473 D, εὐδαιμονιζόμενος ὑπὸ τῶν πολιτῶν καὶ τῶν ἄλλων ξένων.

C ἐνταῦθα] Put here for ἐνταυθοῖ, as shown by the relative which follows.

ἐπὶ δὲ τὸ ἰὼν εὐεργετεῖν] The use of the nominative between τό and its infinitive is quite usual Cp, for instance, Rep 526 B, ὅμως εἴς γε τὸ ὀξύτεροι αὐτοὶ αὑτῶν γίγνεσθαι πάντες ἐπιδιδόασιν

ἐνταῦθα ᾖα] These words are part of the text and have to be supplied mentally, if they are omitted. The whole passage from ἡγησάμενος down may be rendered thus—'Thinking myself in reality too honest a man to have recourse to these with safety, I accordingly did not have recourse thereto; for, if I had, I should have been likely to have been no use either to you or to myself· but to going to each of you in private and conferring upon you the greatest benefit, as I maintain, to that I did have recourse'

πρότερον . . πρίν] πρότερον is redundant when πρίν follows; but the combination of the two is quite usual.

D καὶ ταῦτά γε] 'And that too,' representing παθεῖν above.

τοιοῦτον, ὅ τι] 'Of such a kind as would be suitable to me' The indefinite, instead of the simple, relative, imparts vagueness to the expression.

ὅ τι μᾶλλον πρέπει . . . οὕτως] Grammatical consistency would require either μᾶλλον ἤ or οὕτως ὡς. For a similar combination of the comparative with the demonstrative construction see Rep. 526 C, ἅ γε μείζω πόνον παρέχει μανθάνοντι καὶ μελετῶντι, οὐκ ἂν ῥᾳδίως οὐδὲ πολλὰ ἂν εὕροις ὡς τοῦτο See Riddell, Digest § 164.

πρυτανείῳ] Every Greek city had a πρυτανεῖον or town-hall, serving as a hearth and home to the corporate life of the community. It was here that state banquets were given, ambassadors entertained, and pensioners supported See Liddell and Scott, where abundant references are given. The town-hall at Athens, or part of it, was called Θόλος. See note on 32 C, τὴν θόλον.

σιτεῖσθαι] Riddell quotes Dem. de Fals. Leg. p 446 ad fin, τί δε, δυίητ᾽ ἂν ἐν πρυτανείῳ σίτησιν ἢ ἄλλην τινὰ ἑωρε ν, αἷς τιματε τοὺς εὐεργέτας;

ἵππῳ ἢ ξυνωρίδι ἢ ζεύγει] 'With a horse or pair or team'

τροφῆς οὐδὲν δεῖται] Because such a person was presumably rich. Cp. the phrase οἰκία ἱπποτρόφος and the μέγας καὶ λαμπρὸς ἱπποτρόφος of Demosthenes (De Cor. p 331).

τὸ δὲ οὐκ ἔστιν κ.τ λ] 'But that is not as you imagine, Athenians, but rather as I will tell you' Τό refers vaguely to the sentence preceding. Distinguish this from the use of τὸ δέ commented on under 24 A, τὸ δὲ κινδυνεύει. For the force of the pronouns cp. note on 34 C, ταῦτα καὶ . . . τοιαῦτα

διειλέγμεθα] Theaet. 158 C There appears to be no other perfect middle and passive of διαλέγω besides this form.

ὧν εὖ οἶδ᾽ ὅτι κακῶν ὄντων] In unravelling this curious knot of language we must bear in mind that ὅτι is sometimes used superfluously after a verb of knowing which is followed by a participial construction (e.g. Gorg. 481 D). It is manifest also that ὧν is a partitive genitive. The original construction then may be supposed to have been as follows—ἕλωμαι τι ἐκείνων ἃ εὖ οἶδα κακὰ ὄντα. Then the ordinary attraction of the relative supervened followed by a very uncommon attraction of the predicate. Cp. Soph. Oed. Col. 334, ξὺν ᾧπερ εἶχον οἰκετῶν πιστῷ μόνῳ.

[τοῖς ἕνδεκα] The Eleven, or commissioners of police at Athens. One was appointed from each of the ten tribes, and the odd man was their secretary. The brackets indicate the suspicion of a gloss.

δεδέσθαι] 'To lie in chains' A law term. Cp. Dem. 529, 47.

διατριβὰς καὶ τοὺς λόγους] 'My way of living and talking.' Cp. Gorg 484 E, where the two words occur together again, though the meaning of the first is somewhat different.

τηλικῷδε] Cp. 34 E, and see note on τηλικούτου ὄντος κ τ.λ., 25 D.

ἄλλην ἐξ ἄλλης πόλιν πόλεως] The fulness of the expression imparts a beauty to it.

ἐξελθόντι.. ἀμειβομένῳ] For the interlacing of participles cp. ξυντιθέντι διαπειρωμένῳ, 27 A.

κἂν μὲν τούτους κ.τ λ] Here we have a dilemma, which is of the kind known as the complex constructive—

If I turn the young men off, they will turn me out; and if I do not turn them off, their parents will turn me out.

But either I must turn the young men off or not.

∴ Either they will turn me out or their parents will.

ἡμῖν] Ethic dative 'Pray, will you not be able?'

τῷ θεῷ] See note on 19 A.

εἰρωνευομένῳ] Cp Rep. 337 A, αὕτη 'κείνη ἡ εἰωθυῖα εἰρωνεία Σωκράτους.

38 A ὁ δὲ ἀνεξέταστος βίος κ.τ λ.] The influence of the initial ὅτι extends to this clause.

ταῦτα δέ] The δέ here emphasizes the apodosis, 'This indeed' Cp Gorg 502 B, εἰ δέ τι τυγχάνει ἀηδὲς καὶ ὠφέλιμον, τοῦτο δὲ καὶ λέξει καὶ ᾄσεται. See also note on 32 D, τούτου δὲ τὸ πᾶν μέλει. Other instances of δέ in apodosis are Crito 44 B, 51 A, Phaedo 78 C, So D, 81 B, 113 E; Prot 313 A, 325 C

τὰ δέ] Notice how τά here retains its original demonstrative force

B νῦν δέ—] Supply οὐ τιμῶμαι   Cp Symp. 180 C.

βούλεσθέ μοι τιμῆσαι] 'Are willing to assess it for me'

μνᾶν ἀργυρίου] The sum of 100 drachmae = £4 1s. 3d of our money. The following passage from Diogenes Laertius (II §§ 41, 42) may be merely an echo of Plato. On the other hand it differs enough from the Apology to raise a presumption of independent origin, καὶ τιμωμένων τῶν δικαστῶν, τί χρὴ παθεῖν αὐτὸν ἢ ἀποτῖσαι, πέντε καὶ εἴκοσιν ἔφη δραχμὰς ἀποτίσειν, Εὐβουλίδης μὲν γάρ φησιν, ἑκατὸν ὁμολογῆσαι. Θορυβησάντων δὲ τῶν δικαστῶν, "Ενεκα μέν, εἶπε, τῶν ἐμοὶ διατεπραγμένων τιμῶμαι τὴν δίκην τῆς ἐν πρυτανείῳ σιτήσεως. Καὶ οἱ θάνατον αὐτοῦ κατέγνωσαν, προσθέντες ἄλλας ψήφους ὀγδοήκοντα.

Πλάτων δὲ ὅδε] The Jewish historian, Justus of Tiberias, has preserved or invented an anecdote—how Plato, being a very young man at the time of Socrates' trial, mounted the platform, and had got as far as 'Unaccustomed as I am to public speaking,' when he was shouted down by the jurors (Diog. Laert II § 41).

αὐτοὶ δ' ἐγγυᾶσθαι] A zeugma.   Supply φασί from κελεύουσι

C οὐ πολλοῦ γ' ἕνεκα χρόνου] These words are explained by the next sentence, εἰ οὖν περιεμείνατε ὀλίγον χρόνον κ τ.λ.   Translate— 'It is no long time, men of Athens, on account of which ye will have the name and the blame at the hands of those who wish to upbraid the city,' etc.

ὑπὸ τῶν βουλομένων] αἰτίαν ἕξετε is practically a passive verb = αἰτιαθήσεσθε

ὡς Σωκράτη ἀπεκτόνατε] Chronology is against the story that Euripides meant to reproach his countrymen on this ground in his Palamedes, where he said—

'Εκάνετ' ἐκάνετε τὰν πάνσοφον
τὰν οὐδέν' ἀλγύνουσαν ἀηδόνα μουσᾶν

ὑμῖν] Dativus commodi.   'Ye would have had this happen.'

πόρρω   . τοῦ βίου] Cp. πόρρω τῆς ἡλικίας, Gorg. 484 C; Xen. Mem. IV 8. § 1.

τοῦτο] Notice how τοῦτο here is used of what has gone before, while τόδε below is used of what is coming. What a person is going to say can be known only to himself, so that ὅδε, which is the pronoun of the first person, is appropriate to express it. Cp note on ταῦτα καὶ... τοιαῦτα, 34 B.

μέντοι] μέντοι is not unfrequently used to balance μέν Cp D 10 D, εὖ μέντοι ἴστε: Prot. 343 E, ὥς ἄρα ὄντων τινῶν τῶν μὲν ὡς ἀληθῶς ἀγαθῶν, τῶν δὲ ἀγαθῶν μέν, οὐ μέντοι ἀληθῶς: and again 351 A, ὥστε συμβαίνει τοὺς μὲν ἀνδρείους θαρραλέους εἶναι, μὴ μέντοι τούς γε θαρραλέους ἀνδρείους πάντας. See on this subject Riddell, Digest § 162.

θρηνοῦντός τέ μου] Supply ἀκούειν. 'To hear me, I mean, weeping and wailing'

ἕνεκα τοῦ κινδύνου] 'On account of the danger.' So above, E οὐ πολλοῦ γ' ἕνεκα χρόνου.

ὧδε . ἐκείνως] ὧδε, 'in the way I have done;' ἐκείνως, 'in the way those others do' See note on τῇδε τῇ ἡλικίᾳ, 17 C.

πᾶν ποιῶν] 'By any and every means.' The phrase here contains 39 A the same idea as the word πανοῦργος

ἀλλὰ μὴ οὐ τοῦτ' ᾖ χαλεπόν] Cp. Meno 94 B, ἀλλὰ μὴ οὐκ ᾖ διδακτόν. The easiest explanation of such expressions is to suppose an ellipse of some word like φοβοῦμαι or ὅρα before the μή.

θᾶττον γὰρ θανάτου θεῖ] That is, the soul is exposed to more chances of death than the body

πρεσβύτης] Distinguish this from πρεσβευτής, an ambassador B

ὑφ' ὑμῶν] See note on πεπόνθατε ὑπό, 17 A.

ὑπὸ τῆς ἀληθείας κ τ.λ.] 'Sentenced by truth to the penalty of vice and injustice.'

ἔδει] 'It was destined.'

τὸ δὲ δὴ μετὰ τοῦτο] 'But next'

χρησμῳδοῦσιν] See Riddell's note on the subject of prophetic C power at the point of death. With the references there given we may compare Jacob on his death-bed (Gen. xlviii. 19 and xlix.) See also Phaedo 85 B.

οἵαν] Agreeing with τιμωρίαν understood, a kind of cognate accusative after ἀπεκτόνατε.

τὸ δὲ ὑμῖν κ τ.λ] 'But that will turn out to you far otherwise.'

πλείους ἔσονται κ.τ.λ.] Grote sees in the fact that this prophecy was not fulfilled an argument for believing that in the Apology we have the real defence made by Socrates. But probably to Plato's mind it was fulfilled already in the rise of the various Socratic schools

ὑπέρ] Here equivalent to περί. Cp. Xen. Mem. I. 1. § 17; IV. 2. § 23. E

οἱ ἄρχοντες] 'The magistrates,' i.e. here the Eleven.

διαμυθολογῆσαι] Notice that διαλέγεσθαι is not here employed, perhaps because Plato is about to give the reins to his imagination in 41 A-C. For the difference between μῦθος and λόγος see Phaedo 61 B, ἐννοήσας ὅτι τὸν ποιητὴν δέοι, εἴπερ μέλλοι ποιητὴς εἶναι, ποιεῖν μύθους, ἀλλ' οὐ λόγους· Prot. 320 C, 324 D; Gorg. 523 A.

40 A ὦ ἄνδρες δικασταί] This formula was used once before (26 D), but there it was put into the mouth of Meletus Socrates reserves it for the judges who acquitted him Hitherto he has usually addressed his audience as ὦ ἄνδρες Ἀθηναῖοι, more rarely as ὦ ἄνδρες (e.g. 22 B, 29 A, 34 B, 35 B ad fin., 39 E) or ὦ Ἀθηναῖοι simply (30 B, 33 C, 37 A).

δικαστάς] 'Dispensers of justice'

πάνυ ἐπὶ σμικροῖς] 'Quite upon trifling matters' For an instance see Euthyd 272 E, where the supernatural sign checks Socrates when he is about to rise from his seat

For the position of πάνυ cp Prot 338 E, πάνυ μὲν οὐκ ἤθελεν, 'was quite unwilling.'

B οὔτε ἡνίκα ἀνέβαινον] 'Nor when I was coming up here before the court,' i.e. mounting the platform to present myself before the court. See note on 17 D, ἀναβέβηκα, and cp. Gorg 486 B, εἰς τὸ δικαστήριον ἀναβάς

κινδυνεύει γάρ κ.τ.λ] 'Perhaps this thing which has happened may have been a good thing for me.' Cp. Xen. Apologia Socratis § 5, Ἦ θαυμαστὸν νομίζεις εἰ καὶ τῷ θεῷ δοκεῖ ἐμὲ βέλτιον εἶναι ἤδη τελευτᾶν; The key-note of that treatise lies in insistence on the fact that Socrates had made up his mind to die. Xenophon tells us that the δαιμόνιον hindered Socrates when he attempted to prepare a defence (Mem. IV. 8. § 5: Apol. § 4).

C τεθνάναι] Not 'to die,' but 'to be dead.' Cp. Gorg. 493 A, ὡς νῦν ἡμεῖς τέθναμεν See note on 25 D, ἔγνωκας.

τι ἀγαθὸν πράξειν] 'To meet with some good fortune.'

αὐτό] Referring to τὸ τεθνάναι.

ἢ γὰρ οἷον κ.τ.λ.] 'Either it is, as it were, that the dead man is nothing'

τοῦ τόπου τοῦ ἐνθένδε] This is a pregnant construction similar to such phrases as οἱ ἐκ τῆς πόλεως ἔφυγον. For a well-known instance cp Demosth. de Cor. p. 284 ad fin., τούς τ' ἐκ τῶν σκηνῶν τῶν κατὰ τὴν ἀγορὰν ἐξεῖργον.

D ἐγὼ γὰρ ἂν οἶμαι] This is the beginning of the apodosis, which is resumed at οἶμαι ἄν below, after the long protasis has intervened The ἄν strikes the key-note of the sentence as being conditional, but does not become effective till ἂν εὑρεῖν in E

ὁ πᾶς χρόνος] 'All time,' collectively.   **E**

Μίνως τε κ.τ.λ.] Strictly these names ought to be in apposition **41 A** to τοὺς ἀληθῶς δικαστάς, but they are attracted into the nominative through the influence of the relative clause which intervenes. For a similar instance see Meno 94 D, ἐξευρεῖν ἂν ὅστις ἔμελλεν αὐτοῦ τοὺς υἱεῖς ἀγαθοὺς ποιήσειν, ἢ τῶν ἐπιχωρίων τις ἢ τῶν ξένων, where τις ought to be in apposition to the suppressed object after ἐξευρεῖν. In the Gorgias 523 E, 524 A, Minos, Rhadamanthys and Aeacus are mentioned as holding judgment on men after death Rhadamanthys has jurisdiction over the souls that come from Asia, Aeacus over those that come from Europe, while Minos holds a court of appeal, in case the other two are in any doubt Rhadamanthys is mentioned in the Odyssey (IV 564) as living in Elysium Triptolemus appears only here in a judicial capacity.

Ὀρφεῖ . . καὶ Μουσαίῳ] These two names occur together again in Prot 316 D; Ion 536 B; Rep. 364 E Plato calls Orpheus the son of Oeagrus (Symp 179 D), and quotes familiarly from his poems (Crat 402 B, Phil 66 C, Laws 669 D) But he has not the most distant idea of his date, lumping him along with other early discoverers—Daedalus, Palamedes, Marsyas, Olympus and Amphion—as having lived some thousand or two thousand years ago (Laws 677 D). The legendary history of Orpheus was evidently known to Plato, as he makes Phaedrus in the Symposium (179 D) give a distorted version of it. The magic of his voice is referred to in Prot 315 A, and the sweetness of his hymns in Laws 829 E. In the vision of Er his soul is made to choose the life of a swan (Rep 620 A) The oracles of Musaeus are mentioned in Herod VIII. 96 They were arranged and edited by Onomacritus, who was banished from Athens by Hipparchus for interpolating them (VII 6). Plato speaks of a host of books passing in his time under the names of Orpheus and Musaeus, which he evidently does not regard as authentic (Rep 364 E). At the same time he acknowledges a genuine Musaeus, and criticizes his conception of the future life as a degrading one (Rep. 363 C, D). Musaeus seems also to have written on cures for diseases (Arist. Frogs 1033). The names of Orpheus and Musaeus were connected with mysteries, and were made much use of by a set of priestly pretenders (Prot. 316 D; Rep. 364 E), who declared these poets to be the offspring of the Moon and the Muses. But these followers of Orpheus (οἱ ἀμφὶ Ὀρφέα) were not without their higher side. They practised vegetarianism, like the Pythagoreans (Laws 782 C), and are credited in the Cratylus (400 C) with the mysterious doctrine, with which Plato was so fascinated, that this life is death, and that the body is

D

the grave or prison-house of the soul, in which it suffers for its former sins cp Phaedo 62 B; Gorg 493 E, 493 A) Aristophanes 'Frogs 1032, 3' sums up pretty well what we know of Orpheus and Musaeus.

'Ορφεὺς μὲν γὰρ τελετάς θ' ἡμῖν κατέδειξε φόνων τ' ἀπέχεσθαι, Μουσαῖος δ' ἐξακέσεις τε νόσων καὶ χρησμούς.

ἐπὶ πόσῳ ἄν τις κ τ λ] 'How much would not any of you give?' Notice the repetition of the ἄν, on which cp note on ἐγὼ γὰρ ἂν οἶμαι, 40 D.

B   Παλαμήδει] See note on ὡς Σωκράτη ἀπεκτόνατε, 38 C. Xenophon in his Apology makes Socrates cite the case of Palamedes, παραμυθεῖται δ' ἔτι με καὶ Παλαμήδης ὁ παραπλησίως ἐμοὶ τελευτήσας 'Apol. Socr. § 26).

οὐκ ἂν ἀηδὲς εἴη] These words merely repeat the apodosis which we had at starting, θαυμαστὴ ἂν εἴη ἡ διατριβὴ αὐτόθι It is an instance of binary structure See Riddell, Digest § 207

Σίσυφον] Mentioned here as a type of cunning.

C   ἢ ἄλλους μυρίους ἄν τις εἴποι] The regular construction is broken off as if in impatience See Riddell, Digest, § 257

ἀμήχανον εὐδαιμονίας] 'An inconceivable happiness' Lit. 'inconceivable in happiness'

D   οὐκ ἔστιν ἀνδρὶ ἀγαθῷ κ τ.λ] In this sentence Socrates reaches the sublimest height of Stoicism, tempered with religious faith and hope.

οὐ πάνυ χαλεπαίνω] 'I cannot say I am angry.' See note on καὶ οὐ πάνυ κ.τ λ., 19 A

42 A   πεπονθὼς ἔσομαι] Cp κατεαγὼς ἔσται, Gorg 469 D

ὑφ' ὑμῶν] See note on πεπόνθατε ὑπό, 17 A.

ἀλλὰ γάρ] 'But (I will say no more' for' etc Translate. 'But enough—it is now time to go away' See however note on 19 C, ἀλλὰ γάρ.

INDEX TO THE NOTES.

I. ENGLISH.

Accusative after adverbs of swearing, 17 B, μὰ Δία.
— govd by verbal substantive, 18 B, τά τε μετέωρα.
— of the internal object, 22 C. πάθος ... πεπονθότες
Adverb used as predicate, 30 A, ἐγγυτέρω.
Aeolic aorist, 30 D, ἀποκτείνειε.
Anacoluthon, 19 E, πείθουσι; 21 C, ἔδοξέ μοι
Anarchy, The, 32 C. ἐπειδὴ δὲ ὀλιγαρχία.
Aorist of first attainment, 19 A. ἐξελέσθαι ... χρόνῳ.
Aorist subjunctive forbidding a particular act, 20 E, μὴ θορυβήσητε.
Article, omission of with proper name, 32 B, ['Ἀντιοχίς].
Attic future, 30 C, ἂν βλάψειεν
— optative, 35 D, κατηγοροίην
— pluperfect, 31 D, ἀπολώλη.
Attraction, 18 A, αὕτη ἀρετή; 20 D, ποίαν δὴ σοφίαν ταύτην; 24 B, αὕτη ἔστω; 37 B; 41 A, Μίνως
— of the Relative, 29 B, ἃν οἶδα; 37 B.
Augment, omission of, 36 A, ἀποπεφεύγη.

Binary structure, 41 B, οὐκ ἂν ἀηδὲς εἴη

Cheapness of books at Athens, 26 E. δραχμῆς ἐκ τῆς ὀρχήστρας

Choice of Hercules, 19 E, Πρόδικος
Cognate accusative, 28 E, φιλοσοφοῦντά με δεῖν ζῆν, 39 C. οἵαν
— after adjectives, 20 B, ἀρετὴν
Colloquial language of the Apology, 19 E, πείθουσι
Comic poets who attacked Socrates, 18 D, κωμῳδιοποιούς.
Comparative and demonstrative construction combined, 36 D. ὅ τι μᾶλλον πρέπει ... οὕτως
Compressed construction, 33 D. πάρεισιν . ἐνταυθοῖ.

Dative of advantage, 30 A, νεωτέρῳ; 38 C, ὑμῖν.
Demonstrative corresponding to personal pronouns, 17 C, τῇδε τῇ ἡλικίᾳ; 28 A, ταῦτα; 34 C; 37 A; 38 C, τοῦτο; 38 E. ᾧδε ... ἐκείνως.
Dilemma, 37 D, κἂν μὲν τούτους.
Double accusative after verbs of seeking, 23 B, ἄν τινα οἴωμαι
Drachma, value of, 38 B, μνᾶν ἀργυρίου.

Ethic dative, 30 C, ἐμμείνατέ μοι, 36 B, ὑμῖν; 37 E, ἡμῖν.
Expulsion of the democracy, 21 A. τὴν φυγὴν ταύτην.

Fullness of expression, 19 B, διέβαλλον οἱ διαβάλλοντες.

51

INDEX TO THE NOTES.

Goods, classification of, 29 D, χρημάτων μέν.

Homer as quoted by Plato and Aristotle, 28 D, κορωνίσιν.

Infinitive after relative, 29 C, ἐφ' ᾧτε μήκετι .... διατρίβειν.

Interlacing of participles, 27 A, ξυντιθέντι διαπειρωμένῳ; 37 D, ἐξελθόντι ... ἀμειβομένῳ

Litotes, 17 B, οὐ κατὰ τούτους κ τ.λ ; 19 A, καὶ οὐ πάνυ

Meiosis, 17 B, οὐ κατὰ τούτους κ τ.λ., 34 E διαφέρειν

Negative in Greek, where not in English, 27 E, ὡς οὐ τοῦ αὐτοῦ, 32 B, ἠναντιώθην κ τ.λ.
— in English, where not in Greek, 29 B, εἰ ἀγαθὰ ὄντα τυγχάνει

Nominative between τό and infinitive, 36 C, ἐπὶ δὲ τὸ ἰὼν εὐεργετεῖν

Nominativus pendens, 21 C, ἔδοξέ μοι.

Oxymoron, 24 C, σπουδῇ χαριεντίζεται

Participial clause carrying the force of the sentence, 31 B, τοῦτό γε.

Perfect expressing a state, 25 D, ἔγνωκας, 40 C, τεθνάναι.

Personal construction in place of impersonal, 18 A, δίκαιός εἰμι ἀπολογήσασθαι

Poetry, species of, 22 B, καὶ τοὺς ἄλλους.
— a form of inspiration, 22 C, φύσει τινὶ καὶ ἐνθουσιάζοντες

Pregnant construction, 33 D, πάρεισιν . ἐνταυθοῖ; 40 C, τοῦ τύπου τοῦ ἐνθένδε.

Prophetic power at the point of death, 39 C, χρησμῳδοῦσιν

Puns in Plato, 25 C, ἀμέλειαν

Science and theology, conflict between, 18 C, οἱ γὰρ ἀκούοντες.

Semi-middle sense of the verb, 21 D, ἀπηχθόμην; 35 C, ἐθίζεσθαι.

'Silence gives consent,' 27 C, τίθημι γάρ σε ὁμολογοῦντα.

Similar words brought together, 34 D, λέγειν λέγων, 36 A, γέγονε τὸ γεγονὸς τοῦτο.

Socrates, age of, 17 D, ἔτη γεγονὼς ἑβδομήκοντα
— burlesqued in the Clouds, 19 C
— — on the stage generally, 18 D.
— denied that he was a teacher, 33 A, ἐγὼ δὲ διδάσκαλος
— his aversion from physical science, 19 C, ὧν ἐγὼ οὐδέν
— his campaigns, 28 E.
— his deme, 33 E, δημότης
— his disciples called 'companions,' 33 A, μαθητάς
— his inductive method, 27 B, ἐν τῷ εἰωθότι τρόπῳ
— his intense belief in his own divine mission, 33 C, ἐμοὶ δὲ τοῦτο.
— his μεγαληγορία on his trial, 20 E, μέγα λέγειν
— his opposition during the trial of the Ten Generals, 32 B.
— his poverty, 23 B, ἐν πενίᾳ μυρίᾳ.
— his sons, 34 D, εἷς μὲν μειράκιον
— his tribe, 32 B, [Ἀντιοχίς].
— indictment against him, 24 B, Σωκράτη φησὶν ἀδικεῖν.
— invincible as a disputant, 17 A, δεινοῦ ὄντος λέγειν.
— misconceived by his countrymen, 19 B, Σωκράτης ἀδικεῖ.
— never demanded money, 33 A. οὐδὲ χρήματα κ.τ λ.

INDEX TO THE NOTES.

Socrates, number of his judges, 36 A, εἰ τριάκοντα μόναι
— oracle relating to him, 21 A, ἀνεῖλεν.
— regarded as an atheist, 26 C, τὸ παράπαν οὐ νομίζεις θεούς.
— supported by voluntary contributions, 19 E, χρήματα πράττομαι
Sophists, the Greek equivalent for a University education, 23 B, οἷς μάλιστα σχολή ἐστιν.
— their claim, 20 B, τῆς ἀνθρωπίνης τε καὶ πολιτικῆς.
— why disliked, 19 E, ἰὼν εἰς ἐλάστην
Subject of the succeeding verb used as object of the preceding, 21 F, τὸν χρησμόν, τι λέγει.
Sun and moon regarded as divine beings, 26 D, οὐδὲ ἥλιον οὐδὲ σελήνην.

Thirty, The, 32 C, οἱ τριάκοντα.
— their deposition, 32 E, διὰ ταχέων κατελύθη
Tmesis, 35 D, ἄλλως τε.
Trial of the Ten Generals, 32 B, τοὺς δέκα στρατηγούς

Verbs of perceiving constructed with a participle, 20 A, ἐπιδημοῦντα.
Virtual passives, 17 A, πεπόνθατε ὑπό; 26 A, ἐὰν μάθω, 35 D, φεύγοντα ὑπό; 38 C, ὑπὸ τῶν βουλομένων
Virtue, material advantages of, 30 B οὐκ ἐκ χρημάτων

Zeugma, 38 B, αὐτοὶ δ' ἐγγυᾶσθαι

II. GREEK

ἄγροικος and ἀστεῖος, 32 D, ἀγροικότερον
ἀεροβατεῖν, 19 C
ἀλλὰ γάρ, 19 C; 42 A
ἄλλο τι ἤ, 24 C
ἄλλος, idiomatic use of, 36 B, τῶν ἄλλων ἀρχῶν
ἀμφί, idiomatic use of, 18 B, τοὺς ἀμφὶ Ἄνυτον
ἄν, repetition of, 40 D, ἐγὼ γὰρ ἂν οἶμαι; 41 A, ἐπὶ πόσῳ ἄν τις.
ἄν, with fut indic, 29 C, ἂν διαφθαρήσονται
ἀναβαίνειν, 17 D, ἀναβέβηκα.
ἀναγνῶναι, 19 B
ἀναγνώστης, 19 B, ἀναγνῶναι
ἀναπλῆσαι, 32 C.
ἀντιγραφή, 27 C.
ἀντωμοσία, 19 B.
ἀσπάζομαι μὲν καὶ φιλῶ, 29 D.
ἅτε, 23 D, ἅτε ... ὄντες

ἀτιμάζω and ἀτιμόω, 30 D, ἀτιμώσειεν.
ἄττα and ἅττα, 30 C.
αὐτό, vague use of. 21 B.

δαίμονες, 27 D.
δαιμόνιον, 40 A, πάνυ ἐπὶ σμικροῖς; 40 B, κινδυνεύει γάρ.
δέ, emphatic, 32 D, τούτου δὲ τὸ πᾶν μέλει; 38 A, ταῦτα δέ
διαβολή = prejudice. 19 A.
διατριβή, 33 E, ἐν ταύτῃ τῇ διατριβῇ; 37 C, διατριβὰς καὶ τοὺς λόγους.
διείλεγμαι, 37 A.
διθύραμβος. 22 B.
δίκας φεύγειν, 19 C, μή πως ἐγώ

ἔδει = it was destined, 39 B.
εἰ, superposition of, 29 B, ὥστε οὐδ' εἴ με νῦν.

53

INDEX TO THE NOTES.

εἰ πάνυ πολλοῦ, 26 E
εἴ τις, 18 D, πλὴν εἴ τις
εἰρωνεία of Socrates, 17 B, οὐ κατὰ τούτους εἶναι ῥήτωρ, 32 B, ἠναντιώθην; 37 E, εἰρωνευομένῳ.
— of Attic diction. 19 A, καὶ οὐ πάνυ, 30 C, οὐκ ἐμὲ μεῖζω βλάψετε.
ἐμμελῶς, 20 C
ἐν ὀλίγῳ, 22 B
ἐν τῷ ἑαυτοῦ λόγῳ, 34 A
ἐνδεικνύναι, in law, 32 B
εἰδέκη, οἱ, 37 C.
ἐνταῦθα = ἐνταυθοῖ, 36 C.
ἐντεῦθεν, used of persons, 22 C, καὶ ἐντεῦθεν.
ἐξελέγχω, consr of. 23 A, ἆ ἂν ἄλλον ἐξελέγξω.
ἐπ' αὐτοφώρῳ, 22 B
ἐπεί = though, 19 E.
ἐπιστήμων, etymologically connected by Plato with ἐπιστάτης. 20 B
ἔργω, 17 B.
ἐρήμη δίκη. 18 C, ἐρήμην
ἐρώτησις, at law, 24 C, καί μοι δεῦρο
-ευω, force of termination, 32 A ἰδιωτεύειν ἀλλὰ μὴ δημοσιεύειν
ἔφησθα, 21 C
ἔχειν ἁμάρτημα 22 D

ἡγεῖσθαι = believe in, 18 C, οὐδὲ θεοὺς νομίζειν.
ἠρόμην, used as aor. of ἐρωτάω. 20 A, ἀνηρόμην.

θεία μοῖρα, 33 C.
θεμιτόν, 30 D.
θεός, feminine, 28 C.
θύλος, ἡ, 32 C.

καί, alternative use of, 23 A, καὶ οὐδενός.
καί, expletive use of, 28 B. ὅτου τι καὶ σμικρὸν ὀφελός ἐστιν.
καὶ γάρ = καὶ γὰρ καί, 18 E, καὶ γὰρ ὑμεῖς.

καλὸς κἀγαθός, 21 D
καταγιγνώσκειν τινός, 25 A, πολλὴν γ' ἐμοῦ κατέγνωκας δυστυχίαν.
κτῆσις, different meanings of, 20 B

λόγος, in grammar, 17 B, ῥήμασί τε καὶ ὀνόμασι

μὰ Δία, 17 B.
μαντεία and μαντεῖον, 22 A, ἵνα μοι κ τ λ
μαντεῖον, different meanings of, 21 C
μέγα λέγειν, 20 E
μέν and δέ, duplication of, 28 D, Ἐγὼ οὖν κ τ λ
μέντοι, in place of δέ, 20 D, εὖ μέντοι ἴστε; 38 D.
μή, hypothetical use of, 29 B, ἃ μὴ οἶδα.
μῦθος and λόγος, 39 B, διαμυθολογῆσαι.
μυρίος and μύριος, 23 B, ἐν πενίᾳ μυρίᾳ
μύωψ, 30 E

νή, used in oaths, 17 B. μὰ Δία
νὴ τὸν κύνα, 21 E
νομίζειν = believe in, 18 C, οὐδὲ θεοὺς νομίζειν.

ὀλίγου, 17 A.
ὀλίγου δεῖν, 22 A
ὄνομα, in grammar, 17 B, ῥήμασί τε καὶ ὀνόμασι
ὀρχήστρα, 26 E, δραχμῆς ἐκ τῆς ὀρχήστρας
ὅτι, superfluous use of, after a verb of knowing, which is followed by a participle, 37 B, ὧν εὖ οἶδ' ὅτι κ.τ.λ.
ὅτι, with the direct narration, 21 C
οὐ and μή, in questions, 25 A, μὴ οἱ ἐν τῇ ἐκκλησίᾳ.
οὐ μή, 29 D, οὐ μὴ παύσωμαι.
οὐ πάνυ, 19 A, καὶ οὐ πάνυ; 41 D, οὐ πάνυ χαλεπαίνω.
οὑτωσί, 26 E.

INDEX TO THE NOTES.

οὐ φημί, 20 E, φησί ; 25 B, οὐ φῆτε οὐδ' ἂν ἑνί, 32 A
οὐδὲν δεινὸν μή, 28 B.
οὔτε μέγα οὔτε σμικρόν, 14 A

παθεῖν ἢ ἀποτῖσαι, 36 B.
πὰν ποιῶν, 39 A.
πάνυ, position of, 40 A, πάνυ ἐπὶ σμικροῖς
παρά, of comparison, 28 C.
παρίεμαι, 17 C
παρ' ὀλίγον, 36 A, οὕτω παρ' ὀλίγον
πάσχειν πρός τινα, 21 C, πρὸς ὃν ἐγὼ σκοπῶν
πέμπτος αὐτός, 32 C
πεπονθὼς ἔσομαι, 42 A.
περιεργάζεται, 19 B
περιφερόμενον, 19 C.
πολλοῦ δέω, its constr , 30 D
πόρρω τοῦ βίου, 38 C.
πρεσβύτης and πρεσβευτής, 39 B.
προσκαθίζω, 31 A
πρότερον, redundant with πρίν, 36 C.
πρόχειρος, 23 D
πρυτανεῖον, 36 D

ῥῆμα, in grammar, 17 B, ῥήμασι τε καὶ ὀνόμασι

τά, demonstrative, 38 A, τὰ δέ.
τεθνάναι, 40 C.

τηλικοῦτος and τηλικόσδε, 25 D; 34 E, τηλικόνδε.
τὴν ἀρχήν, 29 C.
τί μαθών and τί παθών, 36 B, ὅ τι μαθών
τινα, omission of, 29 A, δοκεῖν σοφὸν εἶναι.
τὸ δέ = whereas, 23 A, τὸ δὲ κινδυνεύει.
— vague demonstrative use of. 37 A, τὸ δὲ οὐκ ἔστιν.
τὸ ἐπὶ τούτῳ γε, 27 B.
τύπος, of rehearsing past services, 32 A, τεκμήρια παρέξομαι
τράπεζα, 17 C, ἐπὶ τῶν τραπεζῶν

ὑπεικάθοιμι, 32 A.
ὑπέρ = περί, 39 E.
ὑπό = by reason of, 17 A, ὑπ' αὐτῶν
ὑποστέλλω, 24 A, οὐδ' ὑποστειλάμενος.

χρησμός, 21 C

ὦ ἄνδρες δικασταί, use of by Socrates, 40 A.
ὦ πρὸς Διός, 25 C
ὡς ἔπος εἰπεῖν, 17 A
ὥστε οὐ and ὥστε μή, 26 D, ὥστε οὐκ εἰδέναι.
ὡς ὤνησας, 27 C.
ὦ 'τᾶν, 25 C.

INDEX OF PERSONS.

(*n* appended refers the reader to the notes.)

Adeimantus, 34 A, *n*
Aeacus, 41 A, *n*
Aeantodorus, 34 A
Aeschines, the Socratic, 33 E, *n*.
Ajax, the son of Telamon, 41 B.
Anaxagoras, 26 D
Anytus, 18 B, *n*; 23 E, *n*; 25 B, 29 C; 30 B, C; 31 A; 34 B; 36 A.
Antiphon, of Cephisus, 33 E, *n*
Apollodorus, 34 A, *n*; 38 B.
Ariston, 34 A.
Aristophanes, 19 C.
Callias, the son of Hipponicus, 20 A, *n*
Chaerephon, 20 E. *n*; 21 A.
Crito, 33 D, *n*; 38 B.
Critobulus, 33 D, *n*; 38 B
Demodocus, 34 A, *n*
Epigenes, 33 E, *n*.
Evenus, 20 B, *n*.
Gorgias, 19 E, *n*.
Hector, 28 C.
Hippias of Elis, 19 E, *n*
Homer, 41 A.
Leon, of Salamis, 32 C, *n*, D.

Lycon, 23 E, 24 A, *n*
Lysanias, the father of Aeschines, 33 E, *n*
Meletus, 19 B, *n*, C; 23 E; 24 B-28 A; 30 C; 31 D, 34 A, B 35 D; 36 A; 37 B.
Minos, 41 A, *n*
Musaeus, 41 A, *n*.
Nicostratus, 33 E.
Orpheus, 41 A, *n*
Palamedes, 41 B
Paralus, the son of Demodocus, 33 E.
Patroclus, 28 C.
Plato, 34 A; 38 B
Prodicus, 19 E, *n*
Rhadamanthys, 41 A, *n*.
Sisyphus, 41 C
Socrates, *passim*
Theages, 34 A, *n*
Theodotus, 33 E.
Theozotides, 33 E.
Thetis, 28 C.
Triptolemus, 41 A, *n*.
Ulysses, 41 B.

THE END.

OXFORD PRINTED AT THE CLARENDON PRESS
BY HORACE HART, M A., PRINTER TO THE UNIVERSITY

www.ingramcontent.com/pod-product-compliance
Lightning Source LLC
Chambersburg PA
CBHW031349160426
43196CB00007B/785